NOTE ON THE COVER

How do you choose an image to convey the fluidity of gender as explored in a book like this? What would that look like?

The symbols on the cover of this book that surround the title are an attempt to do exactly that. They originated with a discussion among a group of nonbinary Brazilian artists in 2014. The symbols are the result of the group's collaboration, and they are freely available for individuals to use and share.

Because gender is fluid and contested, these symbols may not have the same meaning for people outside this original group. You might have your own way of representing your genderqueer or bigender identity. You might have arranged the symbols in a different order that makes more sense to you.

Trying to come up with an image to convey gender as it truly exists is like trying to reduce a complicated dance into just one frozen moment. It can never be perfect, but it can serve as the beginning of a fascinating conversation.

SHE
HE
THEY
ME

SHE
HE
THEY

For the Sisters, Misters,
and Binary Resisters

ROBYN RYLE

Published by Sourcebooks, Inc.
P.O. Box 4410, Naperville, Illinois 60563-4410
(630) 961-3900
Fax: (630) 961-2168
sourcebooks.com

Library of Congress Cataloging-in-Publication Data

Names: Ryle, Robyn, author.
Title: She/he/they/me : for the sisters, misters, and binary resisters / Robyn Ryle.
Description: Naperville, Illinois : Sourcebooks, Inc., [2019]
Identifiers: LCCN 2018010903
Subjects: LCSH: Sex role. | Sex (Psychology)--Social aspects. | Sex differences (Psychology)--Social aspects. | Gender identity. | Gender nonconformity. | Sex discrimination.
Classification: LCC HQ1075 .R949 2019 | DDC 305.3--dc23 LC record available at https://lccn.loc.gov/2018010903

Printed and bound in the United States of America.
MA 10 9 8 7 6 5 4 3 2 1

To Jeff, my partner in all things.

HOW TO READ THIS BOOK

The strange thing about life in the twenty-first century is that gender has probably never mattered more than it does right now. But gender has also never mattered so much less. How can both of these statements be true?

Gender matters more because it is front and center in our daily lives. We are surrounded by gender as it permeates our world, seeping in through multiple avenues. With the explosion of social media and other online sources of information, you can look at almost every aspect of your life through the lens of gender. You can find cartoons that play with gender by drawing princesses from Disney movies as boys—and the princes as girls. You can watch BuzzFeed videos that portray what it would be like if men were treated the way women are in the gym. In other areas of popular culture, you can read about the lack of strong female characters in movies and on television and in novels.

Politically, you can become absorbed in debates about the status of transgender people in the military and their right to use bathrooms. You can see gender playing out on the global stage through the worldwide celebrity of teenage activist Malala Yousafzai, whose advocacy for young girls in Pakistan made her a role model and a Nobel Peace Prize winner. Gender is there when we go to the polls to vote, when we take to the field to play, when we get up to go to work, when we come home to our families, and when we relax and do nothing at all—gender is still there.

But in other ways, gender also matters less than it has in the past. Though the progress is uneven, many women around the world have more choices available to them now than they ever have before. Many of the strict rules that society has laid out for girls and women are loosening, even if the rules for men are often still fairly tight and confining. Transgender people still face violence and discrimination, but their growing visibility and acceptance has the potential to radically transform our ideas about what gender is. There's no denying that for many people, gender as a concept is changing and transforming. If the gender you're born isn't the gender you end up living, then what exactly is gender, anyway? In all these ways, the grip that gender as a social system has on our lives is gradually loosening, so that year by year, gender matters a little less.

The ways in which gender matters both more and less are connected because they're two sides of the same coin. Evolving ideas about gender draw more attention to the complexity of gender itself as a category. For some people, radical changes

↙   →

to how we understand and treat gender give rise to fear and a desire to keep things the way they are. Gender matters more precisely because of the ways in which it matters less, and it's like that no matter where you reside.

I teach and live in a small town in Indiana. People from the outside might describe it as backward compared to places like New York and other coastal cities. But even here, gender is changing faster than some people can keep up with. In small towns as well as big cities around the world, people have pressing questions about how to negotiate the territory of gender, which seems to be shifting under our feet. The particular versions of gender that have traditionally dominated are fading away, and that can be a very scary thing.

Before I started writing this book, a friend contacted me looking for information that would help a young person who was wrestling with questions about their identity. This book is partly for people like them—people who want a much broader perspective on all the ways in which gender matters.

It's also for the student in one of my classes who is cisgender—meaning that he identifies with the gender he was assigned at birth—and straight and never really thought about gender much at all until his cousin came out as gay. It's for the friend at a dinner party who wasn't sure what it would mean to write a book about gender because she wasn't really sure what gender was in the first place. This book is for anyone who's interested in discovering how much they might not know about something that's so very taken for granted in our day-to-day lives, and for everyone who's trying to navigate the shifting terrain that is gender today.

So let's start our exploration of that shifting terrain with a stupid question (because really, there is no such thing as a stupid question): What exactly is gender?

It seems like a stupid question, but it isn't. People who study gender from a social science perspective point out that gender is kind of like what water is to a fish. We're swimming in it all the time. It's all around us, but we don't necessarily spend a lot of time trying to understand it. Everyone knows what water is, right? And everyone believes they understand what gender is. But do we really?

The perspective we'll be looking at in this book takes all those questions about gender—the ones you thought for sure you knew the answer to—and asks you to think again. How do you know what someone's gender is? Are there really only two genders or might there be more? What is sexuality? What does it really mean to say you're gay or lesbian or bisexual or asexual? How do we sort through the things that we've been told to believe about gender and the things that are actually true? Do we need gender or is it something that we should do without?

Exploring these questions is what we'll be doing in this book, but before we set off on our gender adventure, there's something you need to know. Gender, like many other social identities, is partly forced upon us by the societies in which we live. You didn't choose to be born into a culture that believes that there are two genders instead of just one or an infinite number. At least in the beginning, we don't have a choice about the gender paths that are open to us. In real life, there are a lot of things about gender that we don't get to create. This book, however, is a "create-a-path" book, allowing you to explore how different possibilities interact in complicated, sometimes convoluted ways, to form our experiences of gender. Between these pages, you get a chance to explore what it might be like if all of the many gender possibilities were open to us.

If gender isn't really a choice—because many of the decisions have already been made for us by the particular society we find ourselves in—then you might be wondering why I would write a book about gender in the create-a-path format.

I've been teaching gender to college students for more than fifteen years. Many students—especially heterosexual, cisgender students—come into the classroom on the first day fairly confident that they know what gender is. Pretty quickly, they discover that a lot of their assumptions are wrong; many of the things they believe about gender are simply false. The ground falls out from under them. At first, it's scary, like looking in a fun-house mirror where everything familiar becomes distorted and weird. Seeing the world in new and different ways can be a little scary. But eventually, it's liberating and exciting, like a really good roller coaster, full of unexpected twists and turns. There are places where you'll hold on for dear life and places that make you want to get back in line and do it all over again. I wrote this book because I wanted to share that scary and exciting adventure with people everywhere.

The second reason to use the create-a-path format is that the more you know about gender, the more pathways for living your own gender become open to you. There are a lot of aspects of gender that you don't get to choose. You didn't choose the particular set of chromosomes, hormones, and anatomy that you were born with. You didn't choose your family—at least, not at the beginning—so you didn't get to choose the particular set of lessons your family taught you about gender. You didn't choose your culture and its specific ways of understanding gender. If you've lived your whole life in a culture where there are only two gender options—feminine and masculine—those are probably the only possibilities that you can imagine. You're stuck in the boxes that your society created for you with no way to see what might exist beyond the walls of those boxes. Once you know what's outside the boxes, though, you might begin to plan an escape. Or maybe you'll decide you want to make a new box for yourself.

The more you know about gender, the more gender becomes like a path that you get to create for yourself.

If gender to us is like water to a fish, then you can choose the pond you swim in. You can choose to explore the murky places where the water is not so clear. You can choose to dog paddle or to show off your breast stroke. You can dip your toe in or plunge in cannonball-style. You can begin to see and understand gender for what it is. Some choices will be harder than others, but if you understand the social aspects of gender, you'll see the possibilities; you'll see what could be different. You can make your own path because gender is always changing and shifting.

So, how do you get started? In real life, gender has a lot of rules to follow, but in this book, you're free to make them up as you go along. Navigate through your gender adventure by making your choice and then flipping to the corresponding number at the top of the page. You can certainly read this book by following a path similar to your own, choosing options that are true to your own life experiences. That's one possible route to take: use this book to learn more about your own unique gender adventure. Following that strategy, you'll still learn many new and surprising things about your personal gender adventure. But you should also follow paths that are nothing like your own experience. You may have been born into a society with two genders, but what would it be like if you were born into a culture with one gender? Or more than two genders? The fun of create-a-path as a format is figuring out all the different places you can end up. Feel free to explore all the twists and turns. A create-a-path book isn't usually read straight through, but if that's what you want to do, go for it! It's your adventure, so choose whichever path you like and then after that, choose another and another.

Now, let's dive into the deep end and get started on your very own gender adventure!

1

You are born and so your gender path begins. Or does it?

You might think that the first question to ask about your gender path is whether you're born a boy or a girl. But the first question comes even before that. Some of the most important factors related to your gender adventure began long before you were born. You're born into a particular time and place. Your gender path is going to be very different if you're born into one of the hunter-gatherer groups in which humans lived for most of our history than it will be if you're born in the twenty-first-century United States.

Therefore, the first question is: Exactly how do people in the time and place where you're born think about gender? Or an even crazier question: Do people in the time and place where you're born think about gender at all?

↗ You're born into a time and place where gender exists. **GO TO 10.**

↘ You're born into a time and place where gender doesn't exist. **GO TO 11.**

↑   ↗

2

In the society you're born into, gender assignment happens at birth (or sooner). Unless you are a very unusual newborn, you don't have much say in your gender assignment. As a baby, you aren't able to disagree with the gender assignment that's given to you. Already, choices about your gender path are being made for you.

You also don't get any input into the particular gender categories that are available to you. Maybe two gender categories are just fine with you. Maybe you'd prefer three or one. Maybe an infinite number of gender categories sounds about right to you. Either way, it's very hard to suggest alternatives when you've just been born.

All the same, the culture you're born into will have its own way of organizing gender, and those categories are the options that are available for your gender assignment.

↗ You're born into a culture with one gender. **GO TO 12.**

↖ You're born into a culture with two genders. **GO TO 13.**

↙   →

→ You're born into a culture with more than two genders. **GO TO 14.**

↘ You're born into a culture with infinite genders. **GO TO 16.**

3

Congratulations! You're an intersex infant! You're perfectly normal and you're not alone.

The term *intersex* covers a wide range of reproductive or anatomical conditions that don't fit the claims of sexual dimorphism, or the typical definitions of male and female. Some of the conditions are anatomical and therefore identified at birth, but many are not.

> **INTERSEX**
>
> *n.* /ˈin-tər-ˌseks/
>
> A person who is intersex does not fit the typical definitions of male and female. Often describes a person who has ambiguous (or both sets) or external genitalia.

It may feel a little disorienting at first, not having a pink or blue hat, but being intersex is completely natural. Intersex people like you have always existed. Being an intersex infant isn't the result of any disease or genetic mutation, and it's much more common than most people think. Estimates vary because it's hard to know for sure who is and isn't intersex, but the frequency of all intersex conditions may be as high as 1.7 percent of the global population. For comparison, that's about the same as the percentage of people in the United States who are born redheaded (2 percent of the population). So being an intersex person is about as common as being a ginger.

Intersex is an umbrella term that covers a wide variety of biological realities. Historically, intersex individuals were called hermaphrodites, a word with Greek origins that implies a combination of man and woman; this older term has been mostly abandoned in favor of inter-

> **AMBIGUOUS GENITALIA**
>
> *n.* /am-ˈbi-gyə-wəs ˌje-nə-ˈtāl-yə/
>
> Genital tissue that falls in the gray space between what doctors call a penis or a clitoris.

sex. Some intersex people are born with both a penis and a vagina. Others have ambiguous genitalia—their collection of genital tissue falls in the gray space between what doctors call a penis or a clitoris.

Some intersex conditions are chromosomal, which means that they are located in your DNA—your genetic blueprint. Sexual dimorphism tells us that one of the real and objective criteria for distinguishing between women and men are their chromosomes. Men are XY and women are XX. But some intersex people are XXO or XXY or XO.

Intersex conditions can also involve internal organs. Some intersex people have both an ovary and a testis.

So what happens to you as an intersex newborn? How do

doctors and parents deal with a baby to whom they cannot immediately assign a gender?

A lot depends on the particular type of intersex condition you have and whether it's apparent at birth or not.

↗ Your intersex condition is apparent at birth. **GO TO 32.**

→ Your intersex condition isn't apparent at birth. **GO TO 31.**

4

You've been born a *hijra* in India. You're neither man nor woman, but one of the many gender-variant categories that exist around the world.

Actually, you're not born a *hijra* in India. The *hijra* role is something you become rather than something you're born into. As a *hijra* in India, you get to have some say in your gender assignment, something you wouldn't get in many other cultures.

In order to understand what it means to be a *hijra*, you have to understand a little bit about Hinduism, the religious tradition from which the *hijra* role emerges. Representations of androgyny (the combination of feminine and masculine characteristics) and intersex people (people whose physical bodies don't quite fit into the defined criteria for sorting women and men) are both common in Hindu origin myths. For example, the Rig Veda (a Hindu religious text) says that before creation, the world lacked all distinctions, including those of gender. Men with wombs, a male god with breasts, a pregnant man—these are all common images in ancient Hindu poetry, reflecting this idea of androgyny. Multiple genders are acknowledged among both gods and humans.

To become a *hijra*, your gender assignment at birth starts as a boy. Later, you receive a spiritual call from the Hindu Mother Goddess, known in one form as Bahuchara Mata. If you ignore her call, you risk being born impotent for the next seven future

---

ANDROGYNY

n. /an-ˈdrä-jə-nē/

The state of being neither specifically masculine nor feminine.

---

rebirths—not at all a good thing in a culture where being able to have children is very important. The call tells you to undergo a gender change, wear your hair long, and dress in women's clothes. To answer the call, you join a "house," or a particular lineage or clan of *hijras*. There you become a *chela* (disciple) with a guru (master or teacher) who gives you a feminine name and pays your initiation fee into the *hijra* community.

When you become a *hijra*, you both leave behind your masculine identity and take on a feminine one. You dress like a woman and assume a feminine name. You use feminine kinship terms with others in your house, like auntie, sister, and grandmother. On public transportation, you and other *hijras* request "ladies-only" seating. But you are not truly a woman. Your feminine dress is often exaggerated and, unlike traditional Hindu women, you exhibit a more aggressive sexuality. Part of the *hijra* role involves dancing in public on ritual occasions, which is something Hindu women would generally not do.

You may not be a woman as a *hijra*, but you're not a man, either. Some *hijras* are, in fact, born with intersex conditions. If you weren't born intersex, you must undergo an operation which surgically removes your masculine genitalia. This renders you, as a *hijra*, incapable of fulfilling the masculine role sexually; without a penis, *hijra* cannot penetrate a sexual partner and this makes them not really men, according to the way masculinity is defined in Hindu culture.

Your role as a *hijra* is institutionalized in Hindu society, which means that there are rules and norms about what you can and should do, just as there are for women and men. *Hijras* are ascetics in Hindu society; you are expected to renounce sexual desire, as well as your family and kinship ties. You're also supposed to be dependent upon religious-inspired charity for your livelihood. *Hijras* have a ritual role in celebrating the birth of a son. You and other *hijras* would perform dances to celebrate the birth and then ritually inspect the son's genitals to make sure he's not intersex. You would bless the son on behalf of the Mother Goddess with the powers that you as a *hijra* don't possess: the ability to have children. The family would then give you ritual payment for your performance. You might also perform after a marriage, when the bride arrives at the home of her new husband's family.

Being a *hijra* has its drawbacks. Even with the power granted to you as a *hijra* by the power of the Mother Goddess, you may still be held in low esteem and seen as a social outsider. The *hijra* role is full of such contradictions. Still, as with many gender-variant categories, the *hijra* are evidence that in some places, there really are more than two genders.

↖   To start a new gender journey, **TURN BACK TO 2.**

5

You've been born an *alyha* among the Mohave in North America at the turn of the twentieth century. You're neither man nor woman, but one of the many gender-variant categories that exist around the world.

The process of becoming an *alyha* among the Mohave begins when you're still in the womb, with your mother's dreams. As a mother of a future *alyha*, she would have dreams about objects that are associated with masculinity in Mohave culture—things like arrow feathers. But her dreams would also contain hints of your future status as an *alyha*.

As an *alyha*, you're born a boy, but at around ten or eleven years of age, you start to pursue different interests than the rest of the boys. While they're beginning to practice masculine adult activities such as hunting and riding horses, you play with dolls. Or maybe you play games, like gambling, that are set aside for women. You might want to wear a bark skirt, which is women's clothing, instead of what the other boys are wearing, a breechclout.

Initially, your parents push you back toward being a boy

and doing "boy" things. If you keep it up, though, they accept your *alyha* status and prepare a ceremony to officially mark your transition. In the ceremony, two women lead you into a circle made up of other people from your tribe. Everyone sings a song associated with *alyha*. Dancing as the women do means you're definitely an *alyha*. You put on a bark skirt and are now, permanently, no longer a boy, but an *alyha*.

As an *alyha*, you take a girl's name and insist that all your male genitalia now be identified with names used for female genitalia. You're likely to marry a man as an *alyha* and you won't have trouble finding a husband. In Mohave culture, *alyha* are seen as a good match—perhaps better than young girls.

Once you're married, you'll "menstruate" like other women. For *alyha*, you create the illusion of menstruation by scratching yourself between the legs to induce bleeding. Your symbolic menstruation will be treated the same way as a biological woman's menstruation; all the same ceremonies are observed.

You take on many of the characteristics of being a woman in Mohave culture, but you are not fully a woman. You marry a man, wear women's clothes, and do the household chores of women. But women's lineage names are not allowed for you. And the rules for how your husband-to-be courts you as an *alyha* is also different.

Among your tribe, you wouldn't be ridiculed for being an *alyha*, though your husband might be made fun of for marrying you. You would be seen as generally peaceful, unless someone made fun of you for some reason besides being an *alyha*; in that case, you might respond with violence. You might also be believed to have special supernatural abilities, which could be used in curing illness.

Although the *alyha* traditions are no longer practiced, they are evidence that in some times and places, people who exist outside of the categories of female and male can be given positive meaning and bestowed with some power.

↖ To start a new gender journey, **TURN BACK TO 2.**

6

You've been born a sworn virgin in the Balkans in Eastern Europe. You're neither man nor woman, but one of the many gender-variant categories that exist around the world.

Actually, you're not *born* a sworn virgin. The sworn virgin role is something you become, rather than something you're born into. As a sworn virgin, you get to have some say in your gender assignment, something you wouldn't get in many other cultures.

In order to understand what it means to be a sworn virgin, you have to understand a bit about the historical culture of the western Balkans. Yours is a severe warrior culture that involves blood feuds and murder between competing groups. The society you're born into is aggressively patriarchal, which means that power leans toward men and masculinity. Women have few rights and are seen as social outsiders. Women can't carry weapons, and they are off-limits for violence by men.

At birth, you're a girl. You might become a sworn virgin if your family doesn't have any sons to inherit and carry on the family name. Maybe like Tonë, who became a sworn virgin in the early twentieth century, your brothers die in childhood. With the support of your parents, you become your parents' son. For Tonë, this happened when he was nine years old. You promise never to marry, and you begin to dress like a man. Your feminine name stays the same, but people refer to you with a masculine pronoun. You do men's jobs and chores with your father. Over time, you come to walk and talk and generally move around like a man.

If you're like Tonë, you occupy a wide range of masculine roles in your community. If you have sisters who marry, you're the one who gives them away. You might even command an all-male unit in World War II, which Tonë did until he was captured. Sworn virgins don't marry or have sex because that's a central part of how the role is defined. But along with a younger sibling, you might become master of your own household, like other men. When you die, you'll be buried in men's clothes, but with the blessings of the Catholic Church as a virgin. The funeral oration usually given for men won't be performed at your funeral, as that would violate tribal rules.

Why would you live as a sworn virgin? In this patriarchal culture, you'd probably do it to save your family from the distress of their house "disappearing" due to the lack of any male heirs. Or you might become a sworn virgin to avoid being forced into an arranged marriage. Maybe you enter this role because you always felt like a man, or because you want the greater freedom available to men in Balkan culture. Even if your parents eventually gave birth to a son, you would probably maintain your status as a sworn virgin.

As a sworn virgin, you're no longer a woman, because women are expected to marry and have children. But as you can see, you're not quite a man, either; you don't get the funeral rites accorded to a man. In addition, although you're allowed to use weapons like a man, anyone who attacked you would be stigmatized in the same way they would be for attacking a woman. The sworn virgin role is about more than just gender crossing.

There are fewer sworn virgins like you in contemporary Balkan culture, partly due to the loosening of gender roles for women. Estimates suggest that there are still around one hundred true sworn virgins in countries like Albania. Those who remain occupy a category that is somewhere in between—a gender-variant role.

↖ To start a new gender journey, **TURN BACK TO 2.**

7

Life as a boy in a patriarchal society is pretty good. In a patriarchy, androcentrism is a central lens through which people see the world. Androcentrism is the idea that men and masculinity are superior to women and femininity. Because of androcentrism, you're automatically seen as superior to girls and women, not because of anything you do but just because of who you are. By definition, in a patriarchy, more power rests in the hands of boys and men. In other words, the whole system of gender is set up in a way to benefit people like you. Score!

> **PATRIARCHY**
>
> *n.* /ˈpā-trē-ˌär-kē/
>
> A system of social organization in which power leans toward men and masculinity.

On the other hand, there are costs that come with being on the top in a system like this. As a boy, you're expected to follow all the rules of masculinity. If you don't, even your gender assignment as

> **ANDROCENTRISM**
>
> *n.* /ˌan-drə-ˈsen-ˌtri-zəm/
>
> The idea that men and masculinity are superior to women and femininity.

male won't keep some people from looking down on you in a patriarchal society. If you get labeled a "sissy" boy, you're likely to get made fun of and be bullied. Here's a short list of some things that you'll be discouraged from doing as a boy: expressing your emotions, being nurturing, resolving conflicts easily, being intimate with other people, and taking care of your own personal well-being.

So being in a patriarchal society as a boy is both good and bad.

> **GENDER SOCIALIZATION**
>
> *n.* /ˈjen-dər ˌsō-sh(ə-)lə-ˈzā-shən/
>
> The act of learning how to fit into the particular gender to which a person is assigned.

Now that you know what sort of society you're in, you can get started on the process of gender socialization, or learning how to fit into the particular gender to which you've been assigned. Who does that socializing is important, so you need to know who's going to spend most of their time taking care of you. You need to know who your primary caregiver is going to be.

↗ Your primary caregiver is a woman. **GO TO 30.**

→ Your primary caregiver is a man. **GO TO 20.**

↘ Your primary caregiver is a group of people. **GO TO 26.**

8

You're in a matriarchy. What exactly does that mean? In matriarchal cultures, lines of inheritance and lineage flow through women instead of men. Myths and stories emphasize the power and importance of women. There's some debate about both what a matriarchy is and whether it truly exists. Some researchers argue that all societies we know of are, in fact, patriarchal. But in some places, power does lean more toward women.

In a place such as this, would you be oppressed as a boy? Probably not. True matriarchies tend to be nonhierarchical, which means that there aren't any large differences in social status among people in the tribe or group, even along gender lines. Differences in eco-

> **MATRIARCHY**
>
> *n.* /ˈmā-trē-ˌär-kē/
>
> A system of social organization in which power leans toward women and femininity.

nomic status, based on who has more stuff, aren't important either, because the distribution of material goods is based on a model of economic reciprocity, or a constant circulation of gifts. Mothering is valued in these cultures, so that it becomes a cultural model for everyone. Marriage is matrilocal (which means daughters stay in the household of their mother when they marry), and inheritance is matrilineal (descent moves from mother to daughter rather than from father to son). But the stuff that gets inherited is still distributed equally, so women don't acquire more stuff than men in this system. Because of these patterns of kinship, everyone in a matriarchy is seen as related to everyone else, and this is another way that status differences are flattened out. Everyone in a matriarchy qualifies as a "brother" or "sister" or "mother" within this expansive system of kinship. So you end up with one big family of caring relationships among social equals.

Great, you might say to yourself, *but women still have more power than men, right?* Maybe, but the differences in power between women and men in a matriarchy are much smaller than those in a patriarchal culture, because power is more evenly spread out in general. In a culture where mothering defines how people should interact and everyone views each other as family, decisions are made based on consensus—everyone has to agree before a

---

MATRILOCAL

adj. /ˌmatrəˈlō-kəlˈ/

Denoting a custom in marriage when a daughter stays in the household of her mother when she marries, or the husband moves to live with his new wife's community.

MATRILINEAL

adj. /ˌmatrəˈli-nē-əl/

Of or based on kinship with the mother or the female line in a family.

decision is made. No one person or even group of people (like women) have the ability to tell others what to do, unless everyone agrees. When decisions are all based on consensus, power is pretty equally distributed among everyone in the group. So as a boy in a matriarchy, you might have slightly less power relative to girls or women, but the differences would be pretty small.

As a boy in a matriarchal culture, you might be expected to go live with your wife's family when you get married. Or you might follow the pattern of "visiting marriage," where you don't live with your wife at all. You stay in your mother's household and "visit" your wife or lover, where you're seen as a sort of overnight guest. Your children stay with your wife in her household, and you might not have any rights or duties relative to your own children. Instead, you have social rights and duties to the children in your own mother's household, serving as a "social father" to your sisters' children. Under this kinship system, it's not that you don't have parental rights as a father, it's just that those parental rights are attached to your sisters' children instead of your own biological children.

As a boy in a matriarchal society, we could assume that the person who'll be doing most of the work of taking care of you as a child—your primary caregiver—will be a woman. But maybe not. Maybe in a matriarchy, men are the ones assigned to do most of the childcare. Or maybe men and women share these tasks fairly equally.

→ Your primary caregiver is a woman. **GO TO 30.**

↖ Your primary caregiver is a man. **GO TO 20.**

↘ Your primary caregiver is a group of people. **GO TO 26.**

9

You're lucky enough to find yourself in a matriarchal culture as a girl. Woo-hoo!

There's some debate about whether or not matriarchies actually exist. Some researchers argue that all societies we know of are patriarchal. Still, there are some places where power leans more toward women. So let's assume that you're in one of those places and that matriarchies really do exist.

In matriarchal cultures, power is more equally distributed in general. Because of an emphasis on sharing and decision-making by consensus, no one in a matriarchy has considerably more or considerably less power than anyone else. Because power differentials along gender lines are smaller in a matriarchy, this means that as a girl, you'd have more power than you would in a patriarchal society. You'd be more powerful not only within your own family, but also when it comes to participating in larger decisions about your tribe or group. Property and titles would be passed down from mother to daughter instead of from father to son. Unlike in a patriarchal society where children often take their father's names, your children would be more likely to be identified by your family name. When you are old enough to get married, your husband would move into your family's house, instead of you going to live with him in his parents' house. These and other practices give girls and women more power in a matriarchal society.

Gender socialization would probably still happen in a matriarchy, even if it might be different. Gender socialization is how you learn to become a girl and eventually a woman. The person who teaches you those things—your primary caregiver—is important in determining exactly what you learn. So you need to know who your primary caregiver is going to be.

↗ Your primary caregiver is a woman. **GO TO 34.**

↖ Your primary caregiver is a man. **GO TO 35.**

→ Your primary caregiver is a group of people. **GO TO 26.**

10

Congratulations! You've been born into a world where gender exists! Your gender adventure is under way!

If your parents had access to ultrasound technology, they may be ahead of the game. Perhaps they discovered your gender even before you were born, and your room is already decorated in pink or blue.

Whether it happens before you're born, when you're born, or some time much later, the starting point of your gender adventure is gender assignment. Gender assignment is what happens when someone puts you into a gender category appropriate to your particular culture. To put it simply, gender assignment is what happens when someone announces, "It's a boy!" or "It's a girl!" or "It's something else entirely!"

On the surface, gender assignment seems like a straightforward, easy process. But it's actually pretty complicated. Exactly how gender assignment

> **GENDER ASSIGNMENT**
>
> *n.* /ˈjen-dər ə-ˈsīn-mənt/
>
> Determination by an outside party of a person's gender.

works, and when it happens, depends on the time and place that you're born into.

- ↗ You're born into a culture where gender assignment happens at birth. **GO TO 2.**
- ↘ You're born into a culture where gender assignment happens later. **GO TO 15.**

11

Congratulations! You've been born into a world where there is no such thing as gender!

Wait! Does such a thing exist? Are you still on Earth, or have you somehow been born in a galaxy far, far away? Is it possible to live in a world with no gender at all?

You're not the first person to ask that question, and not everyone agrees on the answer. But if we assume that there are (or have been) places where gender doesn't exist, here are a few possibilities for what that might look like.

One possibility is that gender didn't exist at the very beginning of human prehistory. One anthropologist suggests that in order to understand what a culture without gender looks like, you have to go back in time and imagine that you're an early human being, living as a hunter-gatherer in a small, tribal group.

In your group, you can certainly see that there are differences among people. Some of those differences have to do with genitalia, but you can see many other physical differences too.

There's no particular reason that you would assign more

meaning to genitalia than you would to, say, foot size. Or earlobes. People look physically different in lots of ways; culture
tells us which of those differences are important, and your
hunter-gatherer group doesn't tell you that the physical markers of gender are (or are not) important. Some—but not all—
members of your group who have a certain type of genitalia
can get pregnant. But, as we know in modern times, not all
biological women are fertile, and even fertile biological women
are not capable of getting pregnant all of the time.

If, as a group, you don't really attach importance or meaning
to genitals, then you wouldn't see a reason to organize your
sexual or romantic behavior around them. Babies would still
be born in such a group because biologically fertile women
would sometimes have sex with biologically fertile men. But
this wouldn't be the only type of sex going on. Wanting to have
sex exclusively with people who have certain kinds of genitals
would make as much sense as only wanting to have sex with
people who have round earlobes would. Neither physical difference means more than the other. If gender is the meaning
we attach to genitals and other physical markers, then in your
early human group, there is no such thing as gender. There's
also no such thing as sexual identity (gay, lesbian, bisexual,
asexual, straight) in the way we think of it now.

Another possibility is that gender didn't exist in some cultures around the world before their exposure to Anglo-European

ideas. In places like Europe, beliefs about gender developed in very specific ways. When Europeans came into contact with other cultures, they imposed their rigid beliefs about gender onto them, regardless of whatever ideas these cultures may have already had. For example, among the Yoruba in Africa, seniority (or age) was much more important than any status based on bodily sex or gender. The categories of identity based on seniority were not gender-specific, and knowing a person's seniority status wouldn't reveal anything about their gender. Given this very different way of understanding social categories, did such a thing as gender really exist in Yorubaland before European colonizers introduced the concept? Is gender really a universal category, or have we just assumed that other cultures have gender when what's actually going on is something completely different?

Maybe, rather than gender having been imposed by another culture where it didn't exist before, gender has just mattered a lot less in certain places and times than it does now. Why might that be the case? Some researchers suggest that gender becomes more important when societies shift from simple hunting and gathering to living as settled farmers. Hunter-gatherers move from place to place in small groups, surviving off the animals they kill and the food they find. Everyone is pretty much doing the same thing, so gender doesn't have much meaning. In agricultural societies, however, many different kinds of tasks must be accomplished, so work becomes specialized and assigned on the basis of whether you're a woman or a man. In this context, gender begins to pack a punch. It is true that gender as we understand it now does exist among hunter-gatherer groups that are still around today, but it's much less important, as an identity, than it is in many other cultures.

Others argue that gender becomes more important when societies begin to believe in private property—the idea that individuals can own and have control over land, stuff, or people. From this point of view, gender matters because women themselves can become private property; that is, women become something that can be bought and sold, usually through marriage.

Can you imagine a world in which there is no gender? Or a world in which gender isn't very important? Does it seem strange? Was this the way it was for early humans? We can't know for sure.

For now, every culture and society that we're aware of seems to have some concept of gender, even though there's a lot of variation in what gender looks like.

↖ Sorry, but it looks like there's no escaping gender just yet.
   GO TO 10.

12

You've been born into a society with one gender, which might seem pretty weird. Where, exactly, are you?

If you're in a one-gender system, you're somewhere in the Western world, but you've moved back in time. Some historians of gender suggest that if you were born before the eighteenth century in Europe, you were probably born into a one-gender system.

The one-gender system dates back to ancient Greek culture. The ancient Greeks didn't think of men and women as completely different types of people based on their biology. There was no sense of the "opposite sex." Women were considered lesser versions of men, in the same way that men were lesser versions of the gods. Gender was viewed as a continuum, with gods at the top and women, slaves, and other undesirables at the bottom.

For all that wide swath of history from ancient Greek civilization up until the eighteenth century, it's not as if people were ignorant about human anatomy, both internal and external. They had performed dissections to study the inside of women's and men's bodies in great detail. But in a one-gender system, penises and vaginas are seen as the same organ, as are testes and ovaries. In men, penises are external and in women, they're internal—that is, a vagina is an internal penis and not an entirely different organ. In other words, penises and vaginas are different versions of the same thing. An ovary is just a lesser version of a testis. In some sense, a man is a woman turned inside out.

How, you might be wondering, could people have gotten gender so wrong for so long? Were they that stupid? No, they weren't. Greek physicians knew a great deal about human anatomy. The difference lies in how they understood gender culturally. If you live in a culture that believes there is only one gender, then that is the lens through which you'll understand anatomy. Because ancient Greek physicians believed there was only one gender, they saw only different types of the same organ. Today, because we believe in two genders, we see two completely different organs. To say that we're right and the Greeks were wrong is an example of ethnocentrism, or assuming that the perspective of your own culture is correct while everyone else is wrong.

ETHNOCENTRISM

n. / ˌeth-nō-ˈsen-ˌtri-zəm/

The belief or attitude that one's own culture is normal and therefore superior to all others.

Inequality still exists in a one-gender system, it just takes a different form. As a woman, you're inferior not because you're completely different, biologically speaking, from men. You're inferior because you're a less perfect version of men.

↖ To start a new gender journey, **TURN BACK TO 2.**

13

You've been born into a society with two genders, which might seem pretty weird. Where, exactly, are you?

You were probably born somewhere in the Western world after the eighteenth century. From about the eighteenth century on, people in Europe and parts of the world under European influence came to believe in sexual dimorphism. Sexual dimorphism is the belief that there are two discrete and objectively real biological categories called male and female. *Discrete* means that you can only be in one category or the other; you can't be both male and female at the same time. *Objectively real* means

SEXUAL DIMORPHISM
n. /ˈsek-sh(ə-)wəl (ˌ)dī-ˈmȯr-ˌfi-zəm/
The belief that there are two discrete and objectively real biological categories called male and female.

that anyone could look at the criteria you've developed to sort people into two categories and would come to the exact same conclusion about which category you belong to. Your mom and your sister, but also someone from the other side of the world—all of them would be able to use the criteria laid out to sort people into either women or men, and they'd all come to the exact same conclusion every time.

What are these criteria that your mom and your sister are going to be using to assign someone to one gender or another? How does the person doing the gender assignment know whether you're a boy or a girl or something else?

If you're born in the contemporary United States, genitalia are the criteria used to assign you to a gender. You're born, and the first thing your doctor looks for is a penis. If your mother had an ultrasound before you were born, a penis is what the doctor was looking for in those blurry images.

As far as criteria for deciding your gender, the presence or absence of a penis seems fairly straightforward. If you have a penis, then you're a man. If you don't, then you're a woman. The tension in the delivery room is thick. Everyone's waiting with baited breath for the big reveal.

But what if it isn't quite as easy as it sounds? Imagine that you're born and instead of saying, "It's a boy!" or "It's a girl!" the doctor says, "I'm not sure." What happens then?

Doctors are unlikely to tell new parents that they're unsure of what the gender of their child is; they understand how upsetting that answer would be for a lot of parents to hear. But uncertainties do sometimes arise during these first moments in the delivery room.

↑ ↗

The answer centers around one question—what's the difference between a penis and clitoris?

Surely, you think as you're handed off to the nurse to get cleaned, poked, and prodded, *my doctor can tell the difference between a penis and a clitoris. She's a trained healthcare professional, after all, and they're completely different body parts, right? Penises are what boys and men have; clitorises are what girls and women have. It's not that complicated, is it?* It might seem that way, but they're not quite as different as you think. The penis and the clitoris are homologous organs, which means that they're different versions of the same basic, biological structure.

Just a few short months before you were born, you didn't have a penis or a clitoris. For the first eight or nine weeks inside your mother's womb, there were no anatomical differences between you and a fetus of a different gender. You had what's called a genital tubercle, a body of tissue present in mammalian species (like humans) that, depending on the release of various hormones, becomes either a penis or a clitoris.

GENITAL TUBERCLE

n. /ˈje-nə-tᵊl ˈtü-bər-kəl/

A body of tissue present in the development of the reproductive system. It eventually develops into either a penis or a clitoris.

Because penises and clitorises emerge from the same body of tissue, telling the difference between the two of them is harder than you think. How will the doctor decide what to call your particular collection of tissue? Strange as it may sound, she'll probably do some measuring.

→ Your body of genital tissue is longer than two and a half centimeters. **GO TO 21.**

↖ Your body of genital tissue is shorter than one centimeter. **GO TO 22.**

↘ Your body of genital tissue is somewhere between one and two and a half centimeters in length. **GO TO 3.**

14

You've been born into a society with more than two genders, which might seem pretty weird. Where, exactly, are you?

If you're in a culture with more than two genders, there are quite a few places you could be. In fact, *gender-variant categories*, the term used to describe systems that don't follow a strict division of the world into women and men, are fairly common across many cultures. You don't have to travel that far to find a place with more than two gender categories, although the particular characteristics of third-gender categories vary a great deal.

Gender-variant categories exist in some form or another in places like the Balkans, Brazil, Hawaii, India, Japan, Nepal, New Zealand, Pakistan, and Thailand, to name a few. They also exist among some Native American groups in North America.

But let's narrow down the list for the sake of time.

> **GENDER-VARIANT CATEGORY**
>
> *n.* /ˈjen-dər ˈver-ē-ənt ˈka-tə-ˌgȯr-ēs/
>
> A gender identity or gender status that departs from a dimorphic view of male and female.

You've got your whole gendered life ahead of you, and you're impatient to get started.

↗ You were born a *hijra* in India. **GO TO 4.**

↖ You were born an *alyha* among the Mohave. **GO TO 5.**

↘ You were born a sworn virgin in the Balkans. **GO TO 6.**

15

In the particular time and place you've been born into, gender assignment doesn't happen when you're born, but at some later point.

What? No one decides for you whether you're a girl or a boy when you're born? How is that possible?

In some cultures, children aren't thought of as being fully gendered until later in life, often after some kind of initiation ritual. For example, among the Awa people of New Guinea, boys must undergo a series of rituals to "dry out" their bodies, as they believe excess moisture will make it impossible for the boys to mature physically into men. Part of these rituals involve induced bleeding, without which the Awa believe the boys will fail to physically become men. Elsewhere, the Sambia people of Papua New Guinea believe that boys aren't born with *jerungdu*, the essential substance that makes them men. They don't become men until later in life when they ingest *jerungdu* in a ritual setting.

In cultures like these, gender is seen much more as something that you achieve or accomplish, rather than as something that you're assigned. Gender isn't based solely on biological characteristics like genitalia, hormones, or chromosomes.

If you didn't grow up in one of these cultures, you might be tempted to dismiss their notions of gender as wrong or weird. In fact, they're just different. As you continue on your gender path, you'll see that there are things about every culture's way of understanding gender that don't make perfect sense when you look at them up close. If you were born into a culture where gender assignment happens later in life, it would seem perfectly natural to you.

↗ Your gender assignment is male or masculine. **GO TO 23.**

↖ Your gender assignment is female or feminine. **GO TO 24.**

→ Your gender assignment is something else. **GO TO 14.**

16

You've been born into a society with infinite genders, which might seem pretty weird. Where, exactly, are you?

Right now, the possibility of infinite genders is a way of understanding gender rather than an actual cultural gender system. Infinite genders is a mind-set, so while you might be in a place that claims to have only one gender or two genders, you've seen through that illusion to the more complicated truth of the situation—the number of possibilities for gender categories is really endless.

Say you're a woman, which means you're supposed to act feminine. Do you? Do you act feminine all the time, or do you sometimes break the gender rules? Do you act more competitive than you're supposed to or curse too much or smile too little?

Look around you at all the other people who are also women. Are you exactly alike? Do you demonstrate your femininity in the same way? Are you at least more similar to the other people called women than you are to the other people called men? If you're not, what's the point of calling you a woman and calling those other people men?

Maybe one truth about gender is that no one can live out a perfect version, regardless of how your particular culture lays out the rules. As transgender activist Kate Bornstein says, sometimes the gender system lets all of us down.

If we're not all doing the exact same version of gender, if all of us are out of step at one time or another, are we all really doing the same gender? Or would it make more sense to say that we're all doing our own, very unique, versions of gender? Instead of saying your gender is man or woman, maybe it would make more sense to say your gender is Abdul or Maria. Your gender is as special and distinctive as your name. Your gender is as unique as you are.

And maybe, to make things even more interesting, we're doing a different gender depending on the time of year. Or the day of the week. Or the hour. The gender you're doing at lunch is completely different than the gender you're doing come bedtime.

As far as we know, there aren't any cultural gender systems that treat gender as infinite, unique, and fluid right now. But maybe there could be someday in the future.

↖ To start a new gender journey, TURN BACK TO 2.

17

What it means to be a socialized as a girl is going to be very different depending on the time and place in which you find yourself. Gender socialization for girls is the process of learning how to be feminine, but how does your culture decide what femininity is?

That's a question that Margaret Mead, a famous twentieth-century anthropologist, was interested in answering. At the time, most of her fellow anthropologists believed that gender was hardwired. That is, they believed that what it meant to be a man or a woman was built into our biological makeup, so that the rules for masculinity and femininity were fixed and unchanging across time and place. Mead suspected that this was wrong, so she headed to Papua New Guinea, an island in the southwest Pacific, to study a diverse group of tribes living there.

The Mundugumor were one of those tribes. If you were a girl among the Mundugumor, you'd find that people in your culture don't make many important distinctions between what it means to be a boy or a girl. They hold up the same basic set of ideals for everyone, regardless of their gender.

The characteristics that are most highly valued among the Mundugumor include violence, competitiveness, being jealous, and being ready to take action and fight. As a girl being socialized among the Mundugumor, you'll be rewarded for getting into fights and punished for behaving in too weak or passive a manner. You'll be expected to act in ways that, from the perspective of someone from the contemporary United States, would be viewed as masculine.

↖ To explore a different gender path, **TURN BACK TO 2.**

18

Your gender is nonbinary (NB), which means that your gender is not exclusively masculine or feminine. You might also describe yourself as genderqueer (your gender is "queer" or non-normative) or gender nonconforming. You think of your gender identity as escaping from the binary of woman and man or female and male.

It's important to distinguish the difference between being genderqueer and being queer. *Genderqueer* refers to your gender identity, while *queer* refers to your sexual orientation. One way to think about it is that sexual identity is who you want to go to bed with, while gender identity is who you want to be when you go to bed.

As a nonbinary or genderqueer person, the possibilities for your gender expression are wide open. Maybe you look mostly like a woman or mostly like a man. Perhaps you dress mostly as a man but also wear lipstick and paint your nails. Perhaps you

---

NONBINARY

adj. / ˌnän-ˈbī-nə-rē/

Of a gender that is not exclusively masculine or feminine.

appear androgynous, dressing and interacting with people in a style that makes it difficult for them to identify exactly what your gender is. For you, that might be the whole idea.

Though your identity fits under the larger gender-expansive umbrella, you're different from many trans-

> **GENDERQUEER**
>
> *adj.* /ˈjen-dər-ˌkwir/
>
> Being a person whose gender identity cannot be categorized as solely male or female.

gender people. The gender-expansive category includes those who are transgender, but also anyone who expands their own culture's commonly held expectations about gender, whether that means how they express their gender, how they identify their gender, or the norms they choose to follow or not to follow. You don't want to "cross" genders to become the "opposite" gender from the one you were assigned at birth. So if you were assigned a feminine gender identity when you were born, you don't feel that you're masculine instead. You might feel that you're both or neither or something else entirely.

> **GENDER EXPANSIVE**
>
> *adj.* /ˈjen-dər ik-ˈspan(t)-siv/
>
> Describing when one's identity or behavior is broader than the commonly held definitions of gender.

→ **GO TO 49.**

19

You're agender. As a relatively new gender category, exactly what it means to be agender is still in flux. The literal translation of the word means "without a gender." You might think of yourself as nonbinary, which is to say that your gender identity exists outside the binary of masculine and feminine. Or it might be more accurate to say that you have no gender identity. You might describe yourself as genderless or gender neutral or simply lacking a gender.

↖ **GO TO 49.**

20

Though it's been a fairly rare thing in the past and still is in the present, you have a man as your primary caregiver. He'll be teaching you a lot about what it means to be masculine.

Historically and in most cultures, women have been the primary caregivers, either singly or in groups. We don't know as much about what happens to your gender identity when your primary caregiver is a man. In fact, we know more about how being the primary caregiver changes the men doing the caregiving than we know about how it affects children. In the first three weeks after a man's child is born, the level of testosterone in his body drops by a third. Like the hormonal changes that take place in women's bodies, these shifts may exist to help men get ready for parenthood. Studies have shown that men with very low levels of testosterone will hold baby dolls longer than men who are flooded with the hormone, while men with very high levels of testosterone are more likely to engage in non-nurturing behaviors. A study of brain activity demonstrated that men who are primary caregivers exhibit the same pattern of emotional processing that is seen in women who take care of children. So it seems to be true that being a primary caregiver has biological and emotional effects on the men themselves.

What about you, as a boy being raised mainly by a man? Will your masculine identity be more stable because you've learned it firsthand by spending most of your time with a man? Maybe boys raised primarily by men will be more invested in taking care of their own children when they have them. Perhaps the growing generation of boys with men as primary caregivers will significantly change what masculinity looks like. For now, we're not sure.

Regardless of the gender of the person doing the socializing, how exactly does gender socialization happen? There are different explanations, but many focus on the ways in which you're rewarded and punished for behaviors that are considered correct or incorrect for the gender you've been assigned.

What your gender socialization looks like depends on the particular gender norms of your culture. Learning gender as a boy in colonial America will be different from what it means to be a boy among the Arapesh in Papua New Guinea. Both of these will be different from learning masculinity in the contemporary United States.

↗ You're socialized as a boy in colonial America. **GO TO 51.**

↖ You're socialized as a boy in the contemporary United States. **GO TO 52.**

↖ You're socialized as a boy among the Arapesh in Papua New Guinea. **GO TO 53.**

→ You're socialized as something different. **GO TO 54.**

21

Congratulations! You're a boy! The nurse pulls out the blue hat and sticks it on your head. You've only been in the world for a few short minutes and you officially have a gender. Look how much you've accomplished already!

Snug in your blue hat and your blue booties, you might still have some lingering questions. Why two and a half centimeters? Why is that the length at which a newborn's body of genital tissue becomes a penis?

For doctors in the United States, those two and a half centimeters are important because they give an indication of what you can do with your collection of genital tissue. Specifically, a penis is a penis if it's long enough to allow the person to pee standing up and to achieve vaginal penetration. A penis is defined, in other words, by what doctors have determined to be its most important functions—upright urination and one particular, heterosexual type of sexual behavior.

It's worthwhile before we move any further down our gender path to consider these rules for gender assignment. What do the criteria for what makes a penis reveal about our cultural assumptions regarding gender? The most important things that make a man a man are the ability to stand up while he pees and to have a certain kind of sex with a woman. Maybe those seem like okay points of emphasis, but it leaves us with questions about men who don't pee standing up and who don't have penetrative sex with women. Is their officially designated penis going to waste? Are they not real men?

Perhaps your blue hat doesn't feel quite as comfy and warm as it did at first. But you're still a boy, so take some comfort there.

Exactly how good you've got it being born a boy depends on the type of society you're born into. Namely, it's important to know whether or not the society you're in is patriarchal—dominated by men and masculinity.

↖ **GO TO 23.**

↑ ↗

22

Congratulations! You're a girl! The nurse pulls out the pink hat and sticks it on your head. You've only been in the world for a few short minutes and you officially have a gender. Look how much you've accomplished already!

Snug with your pink hat and your pink booties, you might still have some lingering questions. Why one centimeter? Why is that the length at which an infant's collection of genital tissue becomes a clitoris instead of a penis?

For doctors in the United States, that one centimeter is important because it gives an indication of what you *can't* do with your collection of genital tissue. Specifically, a clitoris is a clitoris if it's *not* long enough to allow the person to pee standing up or to achieve vaginal penetration. A clitoris is defined, in other words, by what it isn't. It isn't a penis because it can't do what doctors have determined to be the most important functions of a penis—urination and one particular, heterosexual type of sexual behavior.

You might notice that these criteria are all about defining what makes a man a man and have nothing to say about what makes a woman a woman. In this formulation, men are the norm that needs to be specified. Women are the deviation from that norm. Men are normal and women are not. This assumption or attitude has historically been reflected in the language that we use—in the past (and sometimes still in the present) the word *man* was used as a substitute for all humanity. This implies that the normal state of being human is also to be a man. As a woman, this might have you feeling a bit left out.

Perhaps your pink hat doesn't feel quite as comfy and warm as it did at first. Maybe it's feeling, in fact, a little itchy and too tight.

Exactly what it's going to be like living life as a girl depends on the type of society you're born into. Namely, it's important to know whether or not the society you're in is patriarchal—dominated by men and masculinity.

↖ **GO TO 24.**

23

As a boy, you're probably hoping to find yourself in a patriarchal society, where power leans toward men and masculinity. Lucky for you, you're much more likely to be born into a patriarchy than a matriarchy, where power lies with women and femininity. Around the world and throughout history, there are a lot more patriarchal societies than there are matriarchal ones. But there's an off chance that you might find yourself in a matriarchy instead.

⬈ You're born into a patriarchal society. **GO TO 7.**

⬂ You're born into a matriarchal society. **GO TO 8.**

24

Who has more power in the society you're born into? In a patriarchal society, power leans toward men and masculinity, and androcentrism is a central lens through which people see the world. Androcentrism is the idea that men and masculinity are superior to women and femininity. As a girl, a patriarchy probably doesn't sound so great.

Unfortunately, we know of a lot more patriarchal societies than we do matriarchal ones. In fact, some who study gender argue that all known societies are actually patriarchal. But in some places, power does lean more toward women. In matriarchal cultures, lines of inheritance and lineage flow through women instead of men, and myths and stories emphasize the power and importance of women. Although you'll probably be born in a place where men have more power, there is a chance that you could find yourself in a matriarchy instead.

↗ You're born into a patriarchal society. **GO TO 36.**

↘ You're born into a matriarchal society. **GO TO 9.**

↑   ↗

25

You might not be labeled *intersex* at birth because your condition doesn't include any externally visible signs. That is, your genitalia appear to be within a "normal" range when you're born.

Some intersex conditions don't show up externally. You're not likely to get a genetic test or have your internal organs scanned when you're born, unless the doctors think something is "wrong." So your intersex condition will probably go undetected.

You might end up living the rest of your life never knowing about your intersex condition. Most intersex conditions are not life-threatening and some will produce few noticeable signs. The fact that some people can live their entire lives unaware of their intersex condition is part of what makes estimating the size of the intersex population so difficult.

Another possibility is that your intersex condition could become apparent when you hit puberty. If you've been assigned as a boy, you might find yourself developing breasts at puberty and menstruating, because you have female internal organs.

Either way, for now, you'll live as a girl or a boy, based on the gender assignment your doctor makes.

↗ You're assigned as a boy and remain unaware of your intersex condition. **GO TO 23.**

→ You're assigned as a girl and remain unaware of your intersex condition. **GO TO 24.**

26

The idea of just two people (a mother and a father) being solely responsible for taking care of children isn't the way it worked for most of human history. During most of our past as hunter-gatherers, you would have been taken care of and socialized by a large group of people. This group would have included your mother and father, but also aunts and uncles, grandmothers and grandfathers, sisters, brothers, cousins, and other members of your group. In some places, your mother and father wouldn't necessarily have been seen as more or less important than other people in this group.

In general, it seems that gender identity among these groups was less rigid than it is today. The differences between women and men apparently weren't as important as they are in contemporary culture.

↗ You're socialized as a girl. **GO TO 37.**

↖ You're socialized as a boy. **GO TO 38.**

→ You're socialized as something different. **GO TO 54.**

27

When you tell your parents that your gender identity and your gender assignment don't match up, they might be a little confused at first. "I'm not really a girl, I'm a boy," you tell them, and they insist that it's just a phase you're going through. Or you explain to them that you're neither a boy nor a girl, and they're not sure how to make sense of that. But eventually, they listen to you. They take you seriously. They believe you, and they're committed to doing whatever they can to help. You're lucky enough to find yourself in a supportive, loving family environment, which makes all the difference in the world for transgender and gender-expansive kids like you.

What happens next depends on how you feel about your gender identity and expression. Although the experience of transgender people who have surgery to modify their bodies is the most common representation of what it means to be transgender or gender-expansive, that's not everyone's experience. It might not be yours.

↗ You are a trans man, a transgender person whose gender

↑   ↗

assignment at birth was feminine but whose gender iden-

tity is masculine. **GO TO 47.**

↖ You are nonbinary or genderqueer. **GO TO 18.**

↘ You are agender. **GO TO 19.**

28

You tell your parents that you're not really a boy. Or you tell them that you're a different kind of boy. You might even say that you're not a boy or a girl at all. But when you tell them about your gender-expansive or transgender identity, they refuse to listen to you. Or they tell you that you're wrong. Maybe they ignore you altogether. Or even worse, they yell at you or hit you. Some families kick their transgender kids out of the house. Why?

For some people, gender matters a lot. It is a system that they're deeply invested in, and a set of rules that they believe everyone should follow, including children like you. Among those rules is the idea that you are the gender you're born and that's that. You don't get to change, no matter how bad or wrong it feels. They might be scared about what could happen if those rules changed. If you could change your gender, what would that mean for their own sense of who they are?

Your parents might be afraid of what will happen to you if you go from being a boy to a girl. They might be sad about losing a son, even if they'll be gaining a daughter. They might feel guilty, as if your transgender identity is the result of something they did wrong as parents. They might find it hard to deal with the uncertainty of your gender-expansive identity. Maybe you know at once that you are a girl instead of a boy, but there might also be a period when you're still figuring things out. It might be difficult for your parents to live through not knowing what your gender will be.

As a transgender kid, your power to assert your own identity is limited by the circumstances you find yourself in. If your parents don't support or even acknowledge your identity, it's hard to take action. If you find yourself in a family like this, you might struggle in school. Transgender kids who lack support are more likely to engage in self-harming activities and have higher rates of suicide. If you're lucky, maybe you'll find support in an online community or with a group of friends. You might stay in the closet, hiding your transgender identity until you can find a safer, more supportive environment.

↖ For now, you conceal your transgender identity and live as a cisgender person. **GO TO 40.**

29

Your parents might be a little confused at first when you explain to them that you're transgender or gender expansive. You tell them that you know, deep down, that you're meant to be a girl. Or you tell them that you think you might be neither a boy nor a girl. They're uncertain at first, but eventually, they come around. They listen to you and take your feelings seriously. They believe you, and they're committed to doing whatever they can to help.

So what happens next? Just like there's not one way to be a girl or a woman, there's not one way to be transgender. The dominant media representation of what it means to be transgender is usually someone who "crosses over," most often through surgical or other medical means. But that's just one way to express your transgender or gender-expansive identity. There are lots of other paths you can follow too.

↗ You are a trans woman, a transgender person whose gender assignment at birth was masculine but whose gender identity is feminine. **GO TO 48.**

↖ You are nonbinary or genderqueer. **GO TO 18.**

↘ You are agender. **GO TO 19.**

30

Your primary caregiver is a woman, which means that she'll be doing much of your gender socialization. It's important to examine gender socialization because it draws attention to the fact that very little about our gender identities is already in place when we're born. In other words, we have to *learn* what gender is. Someone or something has to teach us, and the gender of your primary caregiver can influence how your gender identity forms.

Gender identity is how you think about and understand who you are in relation to your gender. It is the way you answer the question "What is my gender?" for yourself. According to this particular theory, if you're a little boy and you spend most of your time with a woman, it becomes a bit harder to learn your masculine gender identity. You're supposed to act like a man, but the person you spend most of your time with is a woman. You might say the first rule of masculinity is to not act like a girl or ever be caught doing anything in the least bit effeminate. So boys learn their gender identity by doing whatever women don't. Masculine gender identity becomes a rejection of everything that's feminine.

Because this is how boys learn to be boys, masculine gender identity has stronger ego boundaries, a psychological concept that comes from Sigmund Freud and describes how we make sense of where our own selves end and the rest of the world begins. Freud argued that ego boundaries are something we have to learn, because babies aren't born with an innate ability to differentiate between themselves and the outside world.

> **GENDER IDENTITY**
>
> *n.* /ˈjen-dər ī-ˈden-tə-tē/
>
> How one thinks about and understands the self in relation to gender.

Because men develop stronger ego boundaries, you're more easily able to make distinctions between where you start and the rest of the world (especially other people, but also animals and objects) ends. Stronger ego boundaries make it easier for you to shut yourself off from the feelings and emotions of other things, including living beings. In other words, because you have stronger ego boundaries, feeling empathy for other people is more difficult for you. Freud considered this a good thing, since it makes you more independent and autonomous.

On the other hand, as an identity, masculinity is less stable than femininity. That means that you might end up feeling like you have to prove your masculinity over and over again, throughout your life. People might talk about something called

your "man card" and believe that it can be taken away if you
don't successfully demonstrate your masculinity. And just like
you learned as a boy, the worst thing you can possibly do as a
man is anything girly or feminine.

The gender of your primary caregiver is important to how
you learn your gender identity. But aside from who's doing the
gender socialization, how exactly does it happen? There are
different explanations, but many focus on the ways in which
you're rewarded and punished for behaviors that are considered correct or incorrect for the gender you've been assigned.
And, not surprisingly, what your gender socialization looks like
depends on the particular gender norms of the culture you find
yourself in. A boy in colonial America, a boy in the contemporary United States, and a boy living with the Arapesh in Papua
New Guinea are all going to have very different experiences of
gender socialization. In each place, you're going to be taught a
very different version of what it means to be a boy or a man.

↗ You're socialized as a boy in colonial America. **GO TO 51.**

↖ You're socialized as a boy in the contemporary United
States. **GO TO 52.**

→ You're socialized among the Arapesh in Papua New
Guinea. **GO TO 53.**

↘ You're socialized as something different. **GO TO 54.**

31

Your intersex condition isn't apparent at birth. Your doctor doesn't label you as intersex, and there could be a couple of different reasons why this might happen.

- ↗ You're born into a time and place where the label for being intersex is different or doesn't exist. **GO TO 33.**
- ↘ Your intersex condition isn't externally visible. **GO TO 25.**

32

Your intersex condition is discovered at birth. This usually means that your intersex condition is externally visible. Intersex conditions that exist at the chromosomal level or that have to do with internal organs are unlikely to be discovered when you're born. Unless there's something visibly different about a baby, doctors are unlikely to do a genetic test or scan your internal organs.

If your intersex condition is discovered at birth, it's probably because you have ambiguous genitalia, meaning that your doctor can't tell whether your collection of genital tissue is a penis or a clitoris. Depending on which direction your doctor is leaning, ambiguous genitalia may be identified as an enlarged clitoris (if the doctor is leaning toward girl) or a micropenis (if the doctor is leaning toward boy).

At this point, your doctor will probably order a genetic test as well as other tests that let her know what your internal anatomical structure is. What she does with all of that information depends on the particular model your doctor follows. There are two different possible models for how doctors and other

↑   ↗

medical professionals deal with intersex conditions. The first is the concealment-centered model and the second is the patient-centered model.

- ↗ Your doctor follows the concealment-centered model. **GO TO 41.**
- ↘ Your doctor follows the patient-centered model. **GO TO 42.**

33

You might not be labeled intersex at birth because you're born into a time and place where people's understanding of genital ambiguity and gender are different. People like you are still born in these times and places, but the meaning given to your body and your gender are different.

People like you have been born with a wide range of genital, chromosomal, anatomical, and hormonal configurations throughout all of human history. Being born intersex is a natural phenomenon. Myths and religions across a wide range of cultures address the existence of people who are neither man nor woman. In Greek mythology, Hermaphroditus, the son of Hermes and Aphrodite, was merged by the gods with a female water nymph, becoming both man and woman. In Hinduism, Ardhanarishvara is an androgynous form of the male god Shiva and his female wife, Parvati, and is depicted as half man and half woman. Jewish legal tradition includes specific marriage laws for intersex people.

Because different cultures have different ways of making sense of gender, they also have different ways of seeing variations in sex and gender. In the contemporary United States, being intersex is generally seen as a medical condition, which means that it's something that needs to be treated with medical measures—like surgery and drugs. But in other cultures, being intersex might be seen as a gift from the gods or a sign of having been chosen for the role by the gods or destiny. Tiresias, a blind prophet from Greek mythology, was a man but was transformed into a woman for seven years, and he was supposed to have special insight because of his multiply gendered life.

In places and time periods with different ways of thinking about gender and genitalia, being intersex wouldn't necessarily be seen as a problem that needs to be fixed. Today, many intersex infants are treated surgically, but this wasn't possible if you were born before the twentieth century. Historical records tell the story of one intersex woman who was born in the nineteenth century with both a functioning penis and a functioning vagina. She lived as a woman and married a man. But she also took women as lovers on the side, because she found sex with women more pleasurable. When asked why she stayed married to her husband, she answered that it was for the financial support, of course. Her life and decisions demonstrate the complicated nature of gender, which is not just biological, but also economic, social, and sexual.

If you're born into a culture or time period that has a different way of making sense of people with bodies like yours, then your body is probably less likely to be seen as something that needs to be "fixed." There might not be any rules laid out for exactly how you're supposed to live. Maybe you'll choose to live mostly as one gender or another. Maybe you'll mix it up. Maybe you'll have your own special status.

Or maybe you're born during a time period when genitalia weren't the most important marker of biological gender. In the nineteenth century, gender was more likely to be determined by the presence or absence of a uterus. Women were people who had a uterus and men were people who didn't. These criteria reflect the values of that time period—being able to become pregnant and bear a child were the most important aspects of gender, so from that perspective, putting an emphasis on the uterus makes sense.

If your doctor doesn't see any reason to pull out the measuring tape when you're born, you'll be assigned as a girl or a boy. You might live the whole rest of your life with no knowledge of your intersex condition. Or signs of your intersex condition might emerge at puberty.

↗ You live as a man. **GO TO 23.**

↖ You live as a woman. **GO TO 24.**

→ You live as a nonbinary person. **GO TO 18.**

↘ You live as an agender person. **GO TO 19.**

↑ ↗

34

Your primary caregiver is a woman, which means that she'll be doing much of your gender socialization. It's important to examine gender socialization because it draws attention to the fact that very little about our gender identities is already in place when we're born. In other words, we have to be *taught* what gender is. We're not born knowing it automatically. The gender of your primary caregiver can influence how your gender identity forms.

Gender identity is how you think about and understand who you are in relation to your gender. It is the way you answer the question "What is my gender?" for yourself. Girls with a woman as their primary caregiver end up with a feminine gender identity. How is that identity connected to the person who spends most of their time taking care of you?

If, as a little girl, you have a woman as your primary caregiver, you get to learn femininity firsthand, by watching and imitating the person you spend most of your time with. You don't have to reject any of the behaviors you're observing in order to become feminine. The strong bond between you and the woman who takes care of you never needs to be broken in order for you to learn to do femininity correctly.

Because of these experiences, feminine gender identity has weaker ego boundaries, a psychological concept that comes from Sigmund Freud and describes how we make sense of where our own selves end and the rest of the world begins. Freud argued that ego boundaries are something we have to learn, because babies aren't born with an innate ability to differentiate between themselves and the outside world. Because women develop weaker ego boundaries, you're less able to draw a line between where you start and the rest of the world (especially other people, but also animals and objects) ends. In other words, you find it much easier to experience

> ### EGO BOUNDARIES
> *n.* /ˈē-(ˌ)gō ˈbau̇n-d(ə-)rēs/
>
> Distinctions that describe how one makes sense of where the self ends and the rest of the world begins.

empathy for other people in your life. Freud considered this a bad thing, since it makes you less independent and autonomous. He argued that, in some ways, women never quite grow up, because they never learn to separate themselves from the rest of the world. Weaker ego boundaries make it easier to feel what other people feel, so women tend to see themselves and the world as interconnected. Freud may have seen this as a bad thing, but many feminists argue that it's actually pretty great.

Some psychologists suggest that our ego boundaries affect

many parts of our lives, ranging from how women and men think about justice to how they communicate. Since you feel more connected to other people, your sense of justice is less likely to be based on objective criteria and more likely to emphasize empathy and compassion, and to take into account the specific context of any given situation. In the area of communication, your conversational style as a woman is aimed at establishing connections. When you tell one of your woman friends about something bad that happened, she's likely to match your story with her own tale of woe. Both of you work to establish similarity and connection—*I'm just like you.*

Because, unlike boys, your gender identity isn't formed by a rejection of femininity, your feminine gender identity is more stable, which means that you're less likely to feel like you need to prove your femininity. Femininity is simply part of who you are. Other women probably won't threaten to take your "woman card" away if you don't demonstrate your femininity correctly.

The gender of your primary caregiver is important to how you learn your gender identity. But aside from who's doing the gender socialization, how exactly does it happen? There are different explanations, but many focus on the ways in which you're rewarded and punished for behaviors that are considered correct or incorrect for the gender you've been assigned. What your gender socialization looks like depends on the particular gender norms of the culture you find yourself in. Learning to be a girl among the Mundugumor in Papua New Guinea will be different from learning gender socialization in the contemporary United States.

↗ You're socialized as a girl among the Mundugumor in Papua New Guinea. **GO TO 17.**

↖ You're socialized as a girl in the contemporary United States. **GO TO 59.**

↘ You're socialized as something different. **GO TO 54.**

35

What happens to your gender identity if you're a girl being raised primarily by a man? Will your feminine identity be less stable? Will your ego boundaries be more rigid? Though there's less research about this situation, some studies suggest that, at least for middle-class girls, having an involved father can matter for self-confidence and how heterosexual girls approach sex and dating. For these girls, fathers are important resources that prepare them to resist pressure from boys to have sex before they're ready, and to place less importance on dating in general. However, this research focused broadly on girls having strong relationships with their fathers. Due to the fact that, across history and in contemporary society, men are less likely to be primary caregivers, we're still not exactly sure how being taken care of by a man affects feminine gender identity.

Aside from who's doing the gender socialization, how exactly does it happen? There are different explanations, but many focus on the ways in which you're rewarded and punished for behaviors that are considered correct or incorrect for the gender you've been assigned. What your gender socialization looks like depends on the particular gender norms of your culture. Learning to be a girl among the Mundugumor in Papua New Guinea will be different from learning gender socialization in the contemporary United States.

- ↗ You're socialized as a girl among the Mundugumor in Papua New Guinea. **GO TO 17.**
- ↖ You're socialized as a girl in the contemporary United States. **GO TO 59.**
- ↘ You're socialized as something different. **GO TO 54.**

36

As a girl in a patriarchal society, you're automatically seen as inferior to boys and men just by virtue of having been born a girl. People will mostly expect you to act in feminine ways and will also see your femininity as something that makes you less-than. You'll be more likely to feel bad about your body as a girl, and therefore also more likely to suffer from eating disorders. Wherever you are in the world, the media will probably depict you as more passive compared to active, authoritative, and in-control boys.

Because of androcentrism, it might be considered more acceptable for you to step outside of your gender and do masculine things than it would be for a boy to do feminine things. In fact, girls are often rewarded for acting masculine. It's seen as much more okay for a girl to be a tomboy than it is for a boy to be a "sissy." That is, up until a certain age. If you're still acting too much like a boy when you hit puberty, you'll probably be told to start being more "ladylike."

So being in a patriarchal society as a girl isn't so great. But exactly how patriarchal is the place you've been born into?

Exactly how much inequality is there between women and men? How would you even go about measuring something like the amount of gender inequality in the first place?

↖ **GO TO 46.**

37

Aside from who's doing the socializing (man, woman, or group), how exactly does gender socialization happen? There are different explanations, but many focus on the ways in which you're rewarded and punished for behaviors that are considered correct or incorrect for the gender you've been assigned. What your gender socialization looks like depends on the particular gender norms of your culture. Learning to be a girl among the Mundugumor in Papua New Guinea will be different from learning gender socialization in the contemporary United States.

↗ You're socialized as a girl among the Mundugumor in Papua New Guinea. **GO TO 17.**

↖ You're socialized as a girl in the contemporary United States. **GO TO 59.**

↘ You're socialized as something different. **GO TO 54.**

38

The identity of your primary caregiver (man, woman, or group) influences how you learn your gender identity. But aside from who's doing the gender socialization, how exactly does it happen? There are different explanations, but many focus on the ways in which you're rewarded and punished for behaviors that are considered correct or incorrect for the gender you've been assigned. Not surprisingly, what your gender socialization looks like depends on the particular gender norms of the culture you find yourself in. A boy in colonial America, a boy in the contemporary United States, and a boy living with the Arapesh in Papua New Guinea are all going to have very different experiences of gender socialization.

↗ You're socialized as a boy in colonial America. **GO TO 51.**

↖ You're socialized as a boy in the contemporary United States. **GO TO 52.**

→ You're socialized among the Arapesh in Papua New Guinea. **GO TO 53.**

↘ You're socialized as something different. **GO TO 54.**

↑   ↗

39

Up until puberty, most of the differences between girls and boys are social rather than biological. In fact, even after puberty, humans as a species have very little gender-based differentiation compared to other species. Think about bird species among whom males and females are completely different colors. A male cardinal is bright red while a female cardinal is brown. Or consider the female hairy anglerfish, who is almost fourteen times as large as the male and looks nothing like him. Or male lions, with their stately manes, and female lions, without them. Comparatively, human women and men look pretty much alike, and this is especially true before secondary sex characteristics develop. That's why, as a girl, you might have been allowed to run around with your shirt off before puberty.

Secondary sex characteristics are bodily changes that are brought about with the introduction of certain hormones after puberty. Before puberty, neither boys nor girls have breasts. Their voices sound the same. No one has facial hair or armpit hair or leg hair that needs to be shaved. Puberty is the moment when both the social and biological aspects of gender become even more intense.

↗ You develop earlier than other girls at puberty. **GO TO 68.**

↖ You develop later than other girls at puberty. **GO TO 69.**

↘ You develop differently from other girls at puberty. **GO TO 70.**

40

Puberty is an important crossroads of sorts in your gender path. Up until puberty, a lot of the differences between boys and girls are social rather than physiological. In fact, in most human societies, it's the social aspects of gender, rather than biological sex, that people use to make assumptions about what gender you fit into.

Think about it. In most places, humans don't walk around completely naked all the time. We hide our genitalia—what we assume are the biggest markers of biological sex—under our clothes. You may think that you can see other bodily differences—the shape of breasts or the curve of a big butt—but they don't always tell the full story. Breasts are easy enough to fake and they're not always perfect indicators of under-lying biological gender. Sometimes men have breasts and often women don't. You might think of a big butt as a feminine trait, but there are plenty of men with junk in their trunk. Before puberty, your body as a boy doesn't look much different from the bodies of the girls around you. After puberty, some more visible bodily differences might emerge. But even then, they won't always be a perfect guide.

↗ You develop earlier than other boys at puberty. **GO TO 91.**

↖ You develop later than other boys at puberty. **GO TO 92.**

↘ You develop differently from other boys at puberty. **GO TO 70.**

41

You're born with some type of intersex condition, and your doctor decides to handle it with a concealment-centered model.

The concealment-centered model is the method for dealing with intersex infants that dominates in many places around the world. Under this model, your intersex condition is seen as an anatomical abnormality which is highly likely to cause great distress for you and your family. Being intersex is considered pathological, which means that you're viewed as having a disease. If being intersex is defined as a disease, the logical course of action is immediate medical attention.

What does this medical attention look like? Doctors argue that if being intersex is pathological, then the correct course of action is to "normalize" the "abnormal" genitals using surgical, hormonal, and other treatments In addition, they recommend that this "normalization" happen as quickly as possible. The reason that doctors feel compelled to act with such speed is the belief that society can't handle gender ambiguity or intersex conditions, so delaying treatment has the potential to increase your trauma. By intervening, doctors believe they are saving you from being ridiculed, isolated, and rejected—even, perhaps, by your own parents.

As its name suggests, the guiding motive of the concealment-centered model is to, well, conceal. The idea is to hide and correct the intersex condition from you and, to some extent, from your parents. The language doctors use to explain intersex conditions to your parents and other family members may be cloaked in so much medical jargon as to make it virtually impossible to understand.

If the goal of this approach is to hide the intersex condition, then, of course, you as the intersex person don't have any say in what happens to your body. In this model, "fixing" the problem must happen as soon as possible, when you're still an infant and therefore incapable of participating in decisions about your body. The concealment-centered model also advises doctors and family members to continue to hide the truth from you when you get older; telling you about your intersex condition would just lead to more gender confusion. Certain medical information and records are likely to be withheld from you as you age. Doctors will continue to use ambiguous language in their interactions with you. If you've been gender assigned as a woman but still have masculine internal organs, they might say something like, "We removed your twisted ovaries," instead of, "We removed your testes."

So if you're an intersex person and your doctors use the

concealment-centered approach, decisions about your body and your gender are made for you when you're too young to have any input. What's troubling to many intersex activists is that many of these decisions are difficult or impossible to reverse. If someday you do find out about your intersex condition and feel that the gender your doctors and parents chose for you is wrong, some of the damage done by surgeries may be irreversible.

For example, if you have a Y chromosome and an "inadequate" or unreconstructible penis, you'll be assigned female and surgically reconstructed as such. This means that your "inadequate" penis is removed. You can see how this would become a problem if you discover later on as an adult that you identify as male.

Intersex activists argue that the concealment-centered model surgically "normalizes" you not because it's in your best medical interest, but in order to force you into society's existing gender categories. Most intersex conditions are not physiologically harmful; being intersex won't kill you and usually doesn't cause any medical problems. The "problem" with being intersex is a social one rather than a medical one, but doctors still use medical solutions.

If you're born intersex under the concealment-centered model, a gender will be assigned to you and your body will be made to fit that assignment as closely as possible. It may be many years before you find out about your condition, if you find out at all.

- ↗ You're assigned to be a boy. **GO TO 23.**
- ↘ You're assigned to be a girl. **GO TO 24.**

42

You're born with some type of intersex condition, and your doctor decides to handle it with a patient-centered model.

The patient-centered model is advocated by many intersex activists but still isn't the norm in most countries. There are currently only two countries that have outlawed "corrective" surgery on intersex infants—Chile and Malta. As an intersex infant anywhere else in the world, you're less likely to encounter the patient-centered model.

Under the patient-centered model, intersex conditions are seen as a relatively common variation from the standard versions of "female" and "male." Sexual and reproductive anatomy are treated no differently from hair color or skin color, in that all of these physical characteristics vary along a wide spectrum. Some people have red hair, some people are blond, and some people have black hair, just like some people have XY chromosomes, others have XX or XO chromosomes, and other combinations are possible too. Drawing the line between where red hair ends and brown hair begins is hard, just as it is for the characteristics of biological gender. Variation is natural, so proponents of the patient-centered model believe that being intersex is neither a medical nor a social pathology. That is to say, being intersex is not a disease and therefore should not be treated as such.

In a patient-centered model, your family gets some support in the form of counseling from experts, as well as from intersex adults. The doctors provide your parents with as much information about your intersex condition as they can handle.

Under this model, nothing permanent or irreversible happens to you until you're old enough to make a decision for yourself. Parents, doctors, and extended family decide together what gender to assign you until you are certain for yourself about your gender identity. This only happens after they've had extensive conversations with doctors, experts, and other intersex people. They choose from the categories of female and male, but they also acknowledge that your gender assignment is preliminary. That is, they understand that later on, you could change your gender identity and alter your initial gender assignment. Maybe your parents decide to raise you as a girl, but as you mature, you realize that you're a boy. At that point, you can pursue whatever surgical or medical interventions you'd like.

There's no attempt in this model to hide the details of your intersex condition from you or your family. There's no sense that a condition that is a societal problem (because of the lack of categories for people whose biology doesn't fit into our existing categories) needs to be addressed through medical intervention. The model acknowledges that intersex people are more likely than the rest of the population to change their gender assignment and gender identity as adults, and it avoids the problem of performing surgeries on you as an infant that are impossible or difficult to reverse later in life.

In the patient-centered model, you're assigned a gender as an infant, but it's not seen as permanent. Those who advocate for the patient-centered model point out that, in reality, all gender assignments at birth should be treated as potentially temporary. No one, intersex or not, gets to decide what their gender is when they're born. Doesn't it make sense to assume that some people might feel later on that the assignment they were given isn't the right one after all?

↗ You're assigned to be a boy...for now. **GO TO 23.**

↘ You're assigned to be a girl...for now. **GO TO 24.**

43

You feel like a girl on the inside (your gender identity), you're labeled a girl (your gender assignment), and you act like a girl (your gender expression). You like the color pink and wearing dresses and playing with dolls. As a result of your gender socialization, you walk like a girl (keeping your feet closer together, as if you were walking a tightrope) and sit like a girl (crossing your legs and taking up less space). You smile like a girl (more often than boys) and you talk like a girl (saying "sorry" more often and using a higher voice). The list of things you're supposed to do in order to act like a girl is a long one. It's hard to keep track of them all. But maybe you do. Maybe you successfully keep your gender identity, your gender assignment, and your gender expression perfectly lined up. What do you win for this amazing feat?

Because of the way femininity is constructed, you don't have to worry as much as boys do about proving your femininity. It's also okay for you to show emotions—like sadness, joy, and caring—which are natural to all of us, but which boys many times have to pretend not to experience.

On the other hand, you get called a girly-girl. Or fru-fru. Or a sissy. Or frilly. Or maybe even weird, all for doing what you were supposed to do. Maybe people think you're weak or a pushover or not very smart, just because you like pink. If this is what winning the gender game looks like, you think it might be better to lose.

The truth is that there is no winning at the gender game. In a society characterized by androcentrism, or the belief that men and being masculine are better than women and being feminine, being feminine isn't really winning. You get bonus points for following the rules, but you're still a girl in a culture where a girl isn't really the best thing to be.

↖ **GO TO 39.**

44

You feel like a girl inside and you were assigned a feminine gender. But you don't particularly like the color pink. You'd rather play with trucks or cars than dolls. You really hate dresses, because they get in the way of doing important things like climbing trees or running or playing sports. Maybe you don't walk like a girl (you don't keep your feet close together, as if you were walking a tightrope) or sit like a girl (you don't cross your legs and take up less space). You don't like smiling (even though everyone's always telling you to) or you have a very deep voice or you don't like to say you're sorry all the time. You can feel like a girl and be called a girl and still not want to do all the things that girls are supposed to do.

Maybe you're like Betsy Lucal, a sociologist who writes about what it's like to be an adult woman whose gender expression doesn't conform to society's expectations. Lucal was assigned a feminine gender when she was born and she identifies as a woman. But she's tall and keeps her hair short. She doesn't wear makeup or particularly feminine clothing. Her gender expression doesn't match her gender assignment and her gender identity, so she's often mistaken for a man in interactions. She gets called "sir." When she uses the women's restroom or the women's dressing room in public, she gets strange looks or is told that she's in the wrong place. Lucal doesn't identify as transgender—she thinks of herself as a woman. She just wants to be a different type of woman through her gender expression, but that's a difficult thing in the strict gender system in which she lives.

If your gender expression doesn't match the other aspects of your gender, you might get punished for not acting like a girl. Like Lucal, you might be mistaken for a boy or man. But those consequences might not kick in fully until you hit puberty, when your parents and friends might begin to encourage you to act more feminine.

Until then, you might be called a tomboy and that's not so bad, especially if you live in a society where androcentrism is the norm. Androcentrism is the belief that men and masculinity are better than women and femininity. In fact, as an adult, Lucal was able to reap some benefits from being seen as masculine. For example, she felt safer in public spaces because people assumed that she was a man instead of a woman. So if you're a girl in an androcentric society, it'll probably be more acceptable for you to act like a boy than it would be for a boy, acting like a girl.

↖ **GO TO 39.**

45

You like wearing clothes that aren't seen as appropriate for men. What exactly does that mean? What are "men's clothes" and "women's clothes," anyway?

If you're a history buff, you know that the answer to those questions has changed a lot over time. As recently as the nineteenth century in places like Europe and America, little boys and little girls dressed alike, and they both wore dresses. It was only at a certain age that boys would put on pants (breeches), while girls would stay in dresses. Boys would (literally) get their big-boy pants somewhere between the age of two and eight. This was called "breeching." Outside of historical examples, you might also know that adult men wear skirts today in places like Scotland (kilts) and India (lungi or dhoti). In the contemporary United States, male priests, college professors, and judges in their robes are all technically wearing a dress, even if it's worn on top of pants. Designers and stores like 69 Worldwide, a designer brand out of Los Angeles, are even starting to come out with gender-neutral clothing lines.

So if you're a man who likes wearing skirts or dresses, there's really nothing strange about it on a global and historical level. But if you're in a place like the contemporary United States, you still might get some looks for your fashion choices. Depending on exactly when, where, and why you wear women's clothes, you might be a cross-dresser or a drag queen. And, no, they're not the same thing.

↗ You're a cross-dresser. **GO TO 63.**

↘ You're a drag queen. **GO TO 64.**

46

Before you can figure out whether you're in a country with high or low levels of gender inequality, you must first figure out exactly what gender inequality is. And that could be hard, since it is a difficult thing to measure. Maybe to you it's all about how much women and men get paid for the work they do; you think that should be the most important way of determining how much gender inequality exists in any given country. But someone else might have a completely different way of measuring gender inequality. For instance, someone else might think that what really matters is how many elected officials in the government are women. Another person might argue that gender inequality is all about women's ability to control their reproductive lives. Someone else might insist that it is determined by the levels of violence against women in any given society.

Given that people disagree about what the most important determinants of gender inequality are, ranking different countries in terms of their level of egalitarianism can get contentious. But international organizations whose goals include reducing gender inequality, like the United Nations (UN), need some way to measure the relative status of women and men. In order to measure how close we are, on a country-by-country basis, to achieving gender equality, the UN developed the Gender Inequality Index. Another global measure is the Global Gender Gap Index, generated by the World Economic Forum, which places more emphasis on women's economic status than the Gender Inequality Index does.

Both of these indexes focus on four main areas—health, education, political empowerment, and economic status. Health-related equality is measured by gathering statistics about women's life expectancy, teen pregnancy, and pregnancy-related health in general. Looking at the percentage of women who have some schooling beyond the primary or elementary level provides a measure of gender equality in education. Political empowerment includes the percentage of elected positions held by women and how long women have been in those seats of power. Finally, economic equality is measured by the percentage of women in the labor force, as well as how their salaries and access to high-skilled employment compare to men's.

In both indexes, the higher a country's number is, the greater the gender inequality. Women living in a country ranked 175 (out of 188 countries) on the UN's Gender Inequality Index, for instance, endure significantly more disparities than those living in a country ranked 25.

So, according to these criteria, how much gender inequality is there in the country you're living in?

↗ You're born into a country with high levels of gender inequality. **GO TO 56.**

↖ You're born into a country with medium levels of gender inequality. **GO TO 57.**

→ You're born into a country with low levels of gender inequality. **GO TO 58.**

47

You're a trans man, which generally refers to someone whose gender assignment was feminine but whose gender identity is masculine. You feel like a man, but that can mean a lot of different things.

Often, when people in the media talk about transgender people and transgender issues, they don't discuss trans men like you. Depictions of transgender experiences tend to focus on trans women, or those born with a masculine gender assignment who have a feminine gender identity. The small number of transgender celebrities—like Laverne Cox, Caitlyn Jenner, and Jazz Jennings—are trans women. Stories about trans men are less common, and as you'll discover, the experience of being a trans man can be very different from that of being a trans woman.

You feel like a man inside, but you might also feel like you need other people to recognize you as a man. You're aiming to achieve social maleness, which means that you want people to interact with you as a man. You need your sense of who you are on the inside to match how other people perceive you on the outside.

How do you go about achieving social maleness, given that at least for the first few years of your life, people have been treating you as if you were a girl? Even though you didn't feel like a girl on the inside, the gender socialization directed at you was all about teaching you femininity. Now you have to figure out how to cross over into the world of masculinity and exactly what that will mean for you, specifically.

You'll probably find yourself in a society where gender is defined by more than simply what kind of body you have. Altering your gender identity can involve a complicated, bureaucratic process to make sure the many documents that record your gender all line up in the correct way. In some states, you can change (or correct) your birth certificate to reflect your gender identity if you have a notarized letter from your doctor stating that this change is necessary to living your life in a way that reflects your gender identity. In these states, you don't need to have any sort of surgery or need to be taking hormones to correct your birth certificate. The same standard is used by the Social Security Administration, as well as the Department of Homeland Security and the Veteran's Health Administration. In other states, you need medical proof that you've undergone gender-confirming surgery before you can change your birth certificate, which presents a significant hurdle if you don't feel that you need gender-confirming surgery. Three states—Idaho, Ohio, and Tennessee—have laws that forbid changes to gender on birth certificates for any reason.

The rules for changing other documents also vary depending on where you live. In some states, you'll have to appear in court to change your gender on your driver's license or other government-issued ID. This makes if difficult if you can't afford an attorney or the legal fees required. Technically, anyone can legally change their name to whatever they want. In reality, courts and other legal officials are often hostile to transgender people attempting to change their name. Other gendered records include your school transcripts. The Family Educational Rights and Privacy Act (FERPA) gives you the right to change your school records so that they accurately reflect your gender identity. All of these changes can be expensive and time-consuming, sometimes taking years to ensure that all your documents reflect your correct gender.

After making all these legal changes to your gender identity, you might feel that, for you, you need to have a body that matches your gender identity. In that case, you'll probably pursue some set of surgical and other medical options. You might also feel that you're okay with the body that you have.

↗ You pursue surgery and other medical options in order to change your body. **GO TO 66.**

↘ You don't pursue surgery and other medical options. **GO TO 67.**

48

You're a trans woman, which generally refers to someone whose gender assignment was masculine at birth but whose gender identity is feminine.

If you feel like a woman on the inside, you may also feel like you need other people to recognize you as a woman. You're aiming to achieve social femaleness, which means in part that you want to look like a woman. You want people to interact with you as a woman. You need your sense of who you are on the inside to match how other people perceive you on the outside.

How do you go about achieving social femaleness, given that at least for the first few years of your life, people have been treating you as if you were a boy? Even though you didn't feel like a boy on the inside, the gender socialization directed at you was all about teaching you masculinity. Now you have to figure out how to cross over into the world of femininity and exactly what that will mean for you, specifically.

You'll probably find yourself in a society where gender is defined by more than simply what kind of body you have.

Altering your gender identity can involve a complicated, bureaucratic process to make sure the many documents that record your gender all line up in the correct way. In some states, you can change (or correct) your birth certificate to reflect your gender identity if you have a notarized letter from your doctor stating that this change is necessary to living your life in a way that reflects your gender identity. In these states, you don't need to have any sort of surgery or need to be taking hormones to correct your birth certificate. The same standard is used by the Social Security Administration, as well as the Department of Homeland Security and the Veteran's Health Administration. In other states, you need medical proof that you've undergone gender-confirming surgery before you can change your birth certificate, which presents a significant hurdle if you don't feel that you need gender-confirming surgery. Three states—Idaho, Ohio, and Tennessee—have laws that forbid changes to gender on birth certificates for any reason.

The rules for changing other documents also vary depending on where you live. In some states, you'll have to appear in court to change your gender on your driver's license or other government-issued ID. This makes if difficult if you can't afford an attorney or the legal fees required. Technically, anyone can legally change their name to whatever they want. In reality, courts and other legal officials are often hostile to transgender people attempting to change their name. Other gendered records include your school transcripts. The Family Educational Rights and Privacy Act (FERPA) gives you the right to change your school records so that they accurately reflect your gender identity. All of these changes can be expensive and time-consuming, sometimes taking years to ensure that all your documents reflect your correct gender.

After making all these legal changes to your gender identity, you might feel that, for you, you need to have a body that matches your gender identity. In that case, you'll probably pursue some set of surgical and other medical options. You might also feel that you're okay with the body that you have.

↗ You pursue surgery and other medical options in order to change your body. **GO TO 89.**

↘ You don't pursue surgery and other medical options. **GO TO 90.**

49

As a gender-expansive kid who doesn't feel male or female, puberty can be a difficult time. If you're transgender in the sense that you feel you were born into a body that is the "opposite" gender from what you really are deep down inside, puberty brings about an unwanted set of changes to your body. If you were born a girl but feel that you're really a boy, it'll probably be disappointing to develop breasts and start menstruating. You might, in fact, take hormones that delay the effects of puberty. This will make it easier to transition surgically and medically later on.

If you're genderqueer, nonbinary, or agender, puberty might still be sort of weird for you. Maybe you feel okay with some of the changes happening to your body but not others. Maybe you make sense of those changes differently from the way cisgender kids might.

What will your sexual identity look like as a gender-expansive person? Many genderqueer people identify themselves as gay, lesbian, or straight, which might seem strange at first. If you're not a man or a woman, how can you be gay or straight, categories that are based on a binary gender system? Perhaps you're a nonbinary person who identifies more on the feminine end of the spectrum. If you're also attracted to more feminine people, you might identify as a lesbian. Or maybe you think of yourself as falling in the middle of the spectrum—as gender neutral. But when you have sex, you have sex as a man who has sex with other men, so you see yourself as a gay man.

↗ You aren't a woman or a man. **GO TO 76.**

↖ You are a lesbian. **GO TO 77.**

↖ You are a gay man. **GO TO 75.**

→ You are a straight man. **GO TO 79.**

↖ You are a straight woman. **GO TO 80.**

↖ You are a bisexual man. **GO TO 81.**

→ You are a bisexual woman. **GO TO 82.**

↘ You are asexual. **GO TO 83.**

↖ You are demisexual. **GO TO 84.**

↘ You are queer. **GO TO 85.**

50

In your culture, people believe that gender and sexuality are connected. In European-influenced cultures, this can be traced back to nineteenth-century ideas about same-gender sexual behavior. In the nineteenth century, scientists started to study the sexual behavior of people. They wondered why some people sometimes had sex with people of the same gender. They didn't call this behavior homosexuality because the word didn't exist back then. The word *homosexual* was first used in English in 1892, and for a while, it wasn't exactly clear what it meant. At one point, the word even referred to people who have sex with those of a different gender.

Most of these early studies of sexuality didn't focus on women's sexuality, which was, not surprisingly, seen as less important than men's sexual behavior. In fact, to an extent, it was hard for nineteenth-century scientists to believe that women had much sexuality at all. What sexuality women did have was supposed to be safely contained within the confines of a marriage and preferably geared toward the aim of getting pregnant and having children. Though there was some speculation that it might be necessary for women to have an orgasm in order to conceive, any scientific interest in women's sexuality was still tied to their status as potential mothers.

During this period, one of the first explanations for same-gender sexual behavior was sexual inversion. This theory stated that if a man wanted to have sex with other men, it was because he was really a woman on the inside. He was an inverted woman. The same would be true of a lesbian, although that part of the theory didn't receive as much attention. If a woman desired other women, it was because she was really a man inside.

Most people no longer think that gay men are really women on the inside or that lesbian women are internally men. But the idea that gay men are more feminine and lesbian women are more masculine hasn't completely gone away. In cultures like these, if you're a gay man, people might expect you to be less masculine. And if you're a woman who does masculine things like having short hair or playing certain sports, people might assume you're a lesbian. In these cultures, we believe that a person's gender tells us something about their sexuality and that a person's sexuality tells us something about their gender, even if this isn't true.

↗ You are a lesbian. **GO TO 77.**

↖ You are straight. **GO TO 80.**

↖ You are bisexual. **GO TO 82.**

↑   ↗

↖ You are asexual. **GO TO 83.**

→ You are demisexual. **GO TO 84.**

↘ You are queer. **GO TO 85.**

51

Ideas about what it means to be masculine change from one place to another and from one time period to the next. So it makes sense that gender socialization will be different depending on where and when you're born. Gender socialization is the process of learning the norms particular to your own time and place.

As a boy born in eighteenth-century America, the two ideal forms of masculinity available to you are the Genteel Patriarch and the Heroic Artisan. Like many ideas about gender, these ideals are specific to social class—meaning, where you are positioned in a hierarchy based on economic resources—as well as specific to the different lifestyles and opportunities available to you.

If you're the son of a wealthy plantation owner, the Genteel Patriarch is the ideal that is held up for you, the model of what it means to be masculine. Your identity is based in the fact that you own land—probably a lot of it. Since this is the eighteenth century in America, this also means that you are white, as non-white people are by and large prevented from owning land.

To be masculine, you are supposed to be refined and elegant. Think Thomas Jefferson, one of the founding fathers, with his carefully arranged hair and fashionable clothes. It is both acceptable and expected that you, like Jefferson, pursue activities that are pleasing to the senses. You might be a wine connoisseur or like to wax poetic about the beauty of nature. You probably even write some poems yourself. It's also okay for you to write long, affectionate letters to other men in which you proclaim your undying love. Men are expected to have passionate friendships with other men that have nothing to do with sexuality and without any sense that this might make them less masculine. Fatherhood is important to the ideal of the Genteel Patriarch too, and you spend most of your time supervising your family and your estate.

If, on the other hand, you're expected to live up to the ideal of the Heroic Artisan, you're more likely to be a white city-dweller. This masculine ideal emphasizes physical strength paired with dedication to budding democratic ideals. As a Heroic Artisan, you're likely to be a shopkeeper or an urban craftsman. So instead of Jefferson with his powdered wigs, think Paul Revere, who worked as a silversmith, a trade requiring physical strength and hard work. The Heroic Artisan doesn't just supervise people, like the Genteel Patriarch does. The Heroic Artisan is also a family man, so you're supposed to be a devoted father who teaches your son your craft. You're economically autonomous, as well; you work for yourself rather than being dependent upon the labor of others, like the Genteel Patriarch is.

Unlike contemporary American masculinity, neither of these ideals includes anything about being violent, or even particularly competitive. The Heroic Artisan is physically strong, but he uses that strength in the service of honest work. There's also no sense that masculinity necessitates the accumulation of a lot of wealth. The Genteel Patriarch was wealthy, but no one expected him to focus exclusively on making more money. These models of ideal masculinity began to change in the nineteenth century, as men felt more pressure to be economically successful and compete with each other. Both of these forms of masculinity demonstrate how what it means to be a man changes and shifts over time.

↖ To explore a different gender path, **TURN BACK TO 2.**

↑ ↗

52

What it means to be masculine changes across times and places, which means that gender socialization looks different depending on where and when you are. The tricky thing about gender socialization, though, is that it works so well that we forget that gender could be any other way besides the particular version we're taught. We assume that the things we believe about gender here and now have always been true and are true for everyone around the world. The truth is that the way you live your gender—the things that seem perfectly normal to you—will look really weird to someone who lives gender in a different way.

If you're a boy born in the contemporary United States, there's a certain version of masculinity that's taken for granted by you and most everyone around you. There are, in fact, rules for manhood that are in place. Four rules, to be specific. The first is "no sissy stuff allowed," which is pretty self-explanatory. As a boy in the contemporary United States, you're never supposed to act like a girl or be feminine in any way. The second rule tells you to "give 'em hell," which means that boys should be competitive risk-takers. It's okay for boys to get in fights, and it might even be expected. "Be a sturdy oak" is the third rule, and it has to do with emotions. Namely, don't show them. Be stoic. Boys don't cry. Finally, "be a big wheel" tells boys and men to be economically successful. Make a lot of money, because he who dies with the most toys wins.

These rules help dictate which of your behaviors people will reward or punish as you're socialized into masculinity. Playing with trucks or imitating action heroes are behaviors you're likely to be rewarded for—both activities fit with the give-'em-hell ideal. The rewards you receive for conforming to these rules of masculinity can be obvious or not so obvious. Maybe your parents will tell you that you're a good boy when you pretend to be Superman. Or maybe they just laugh when you crash your trucks into each other. You're likely to get punished when you do things that boys aren't supposed to do—girly things. If you cradle a doll like it's your baby, your parent might scold you for playing with a girl toy, because it violates the rule that says no sissy stuff for you. If you're too afraid of the ball hitting you in the face to catch it, your parents and others might tell you to be a big boy. Boys, after all, are supposed to be stoic with their emotions and never show fear.

The process of socializing you into masculinity will start early for you as a boy. Your parents will be less likely to comfort you as an infant when you cry if you're a son than if you're a daughter. They'll give you more instructions, as opposed to talking more conversationally to girls. The family stories they tell you will emphasize independence and autonomy, while the tales they tell girls will be all about emotions. Your family will be more likely to play with you in aggressive and challenging ways as a boy. And you'll get a different set of household chores.

You've been assigned a boy at birth and you're being socialized as a boy. That doesn't mean that you'll necessarily end up feeling like a boy on the inside. Gender as a system is set up with the assumption that your gender assignment and your gender identity should match. In other words, the way you feel about who you are is the same as the gender you were told you are at birth. That's how gender is supposed to work, but that doesn't mean that it's the best way or even that it works all the time.

↗ Your gender assignment and your gender identity match up. **GO TO 71.**

↘ Your gender assignment and your gender identity don't match. **GO TO 72.**

53

Ideas about what it means to be masculine change from one place to another. In the contemporary United States, boys are never supposed to hold hands, let alone hug or kiss each other. Boys or men who show affection for each other are likely to be called sissies or labeled gay. But in many Middle Eastern and South Asian cultures, it's perfectly acceptable for grown men to hold hands in public. It's okay for men to greet each other by kissing cheeks. No one's likely to label these men sissies or gay, because that's not how masculinity is constructed in these societies.

What gender socialization looks like depends on the culture you find yourself in. The anthropologist Margaret Mead suspected that this was true, though at the time that she was doing her research in the early twentieth century, the predominant view was that gender was hardwired. Most people, including other anthropologists, believed that what it meant to be a man was unchanging and the same everywhere. Mead went to Papua New Guinea, an island in the southwestern Pacific, in part to examine how various groups on the island had different ideas about gender. One of those groups was the Arapesh tribe.

If you lived among the Arapesh, you would find that few personality distinctions are drawn between men and women—there's little sense that men are like this and women are like that. The qualities that are most valued among the Arapesh are gentleness and nonaggression. These qualities are equally valued for men and women.

So as a boy being gender socialized among the Arapesh, you'll learn to be maternal, gentle, responsive, and nonaggressive. You'll be rewarded for taking care of your siblings and punished for fighting. You will grow up with a set of expectations for masculinity that, from the perspective of a person from the contemporary United States, would be described as feminine.

↖ To explore a different gender path, **TURN BACK TO 2.**

54

Social learning tells us that we learn to be feminine or masculine through being rewarded or punished for certain types of behaviors. Could you use the same system of punishments and rewards to learn something besides femininity and masculinity? Could socialization be used to unmake gender instead of reinforcing it? And what would that look like if it were possible?

You might be born to parents who have decided to try to raise you gender neutral, and if so, you'd be among a growing number of similar families. There are whole Facebook groups dedicated to gender-neutral parenting. If you're born in Sweden, you can even attend a gender-neutral preschool called Egalia. Parents like yours use different strategies, but one method is to not disclose your gender to anyone outside of your family—the idea being that this is the only way to prevent other people from interacting with you in a gendered way. You'll probably have a gender-neutral name, like Star or Storm. Your parents might use gender-neutral pronouns like "ze" or "they," both of which can be used in place of 'he' and 'she.' Your parents will work hard not to reward or punish any behaviors based on whether they're right or appropriate for your gender. So crying when you get hurt and playing with a baby doll will be okay, as will getting dirty and playing with trucks. You'll be able to wear whatever you want—dress, skirt, glittery barrette, or shorts—in whatever color you want, from pink or blue to everything in between. The thinking behind gender-neutral parenting is that children don't really know what their gender is when they're born, so why should everyone try to impose one on them?

If you're born someplace like Sweden, the larger culture might support your family's decision to raise you as a gender-neutral child. In addition to having a gender-neutral preschool, Sweden has made a gender-neutral pronoun ("hen") an official part of the Swedish language. Many psychologists and parenting experts argue that raising gender-neutral children like you can be a good thing. You're not forced to fit yourself into the particular box of boy or girl, and this can give you more room to realize your full potential, making you a healthier and happier child.

In other places, your family might be criticized for their attempts to avoid gender socialization for you. They might be accused of indoctrinating you or inflicting psychological harm. People on this side argue that being raised gender-neutral is too confusing for children, who need the safety and comfort of having a gender identity.

Because raising gender-neutral children is a relatively new phenomenon and still limited to a small number of families, there's not a lot of research to tell us what the short- and long-term effects of being raised gender-neutral might be. One study does suggest that giving children gendered toys prevents them from developing their full range of interests, preferences, and talents. As a gender-neutral child, then, you'll have more freedom to figure out who you are and what you like.

So being raised as a gender-neutral child might give you a head start in life. What happens next? Can you live your whole life as a gender-neutral person?

↗ You feel like you're a girl. **GO TO 39.**

↖ You feel like you're a boy. **GO TO 40.**

↘ You feel like you're neither a boy nor a girl. **GO TO 18.**

55

You're white and your gender identity, gender assignment, and gender expression all line up. That means that you feel like a boy on the inside, you're labeled a boy, and you act like a boy. You like the color blue and playing sports and crashing into things. When you walk, you splay your feet to the side with lots of space between your legs, so you walk like a boy. When you sit, you spread out your arms and legs to take up as much space as possible. You "manspread," as some people might say, a very masculine way of being in the world. You smile like a boy (less often than girls) and you talk like a boy (interrupting and changing the topic of conversation more). It's a long list of things you're supposed to do in order to act like a boy. You might lose track sometimes, but maybe you successfully keep your gender identity, your gender assignment, and your gender expression perfectly lined up. What do you win for this amazing feat?

As a white boy, conforming to all these rules of masculinity will earn you a lot of benefits. You get called a big boy. Or a little man. Eventually, you're just called a man. But even as a little boy, you're given more space on the playground. When you act out in class, the teacher is likely to excuse your behavior as "just boys being boys." As you grow up, a lot of your behaviors might fall under this label, and you'll learn that a lot of things that aren't okay for girls or for boys of other racial backgrounds are more likely to be okay for you. Even as a little boy, you start to reap a patriarchal dividend, which means that you get rewarded for being a boy and lining up with all the rules for how boys are supposed to act. It'll be easier for you to cash in on that patriarchal dividend as a white boy. Which is cool. Does that mean you're winning this whole gender game?

The sad truth is that it's very hard to win at this game of gender. It actually may be impossible. As a white boy, you'll have privileges, or benefits, that you

> **PRIVILEGE**
>
> *n.* /ˈpriv-lij/
>
> An unearned right or immunity granted as a benefit, advantage, or favor.

didn't have to do anything to get. Those same privileges might not be available to girls or boys from other racial backgrounds, but even as a white boy, there's a price to pay for those benefits. You're not allowed to cry, even when things hurt or you feel sad. You might feel that it's only okay to be physically affectionate with other boys when you're playing sports—a quick slap on the butt or punch on the shoulder. You'll feel pressure to see girls and women as objects rather than people, so you might find it hard to have intimate, caring relationships with them—or with other boys and men, for that matter. As a white boy, you'll have power, but it comes with a cost.

GO TO 40.

56

You're born in Syria, a country with a fairly high level of gender inequality. According to the UN's most current Gender Inequality Index, your country ranks 149 out of 188 countries, and on the Global Gender Gap Index, you're 142 out of 144.

The extreme violence and chaos in your country certainly contributes to factors like the maternal mortality ratio, or the percentage of women who die from pregnancy-related causes. In Syria, women die of pregnancy-related causes in 68 out of every 100,000 live births. Like Ruqayya, a woman from northeastern Syria, you might find yourself forced to flee the fighting and violence, seeking refuge in one of the many displacement camps set up for those trying to escape the civil war. Ruqayya was pregnant when she arrived at Al-Areesheh camp, which holds between 3,500 and 4,000 displaced people but has no brick-and-mortar health facility. When Ruqayya went into labor and needed an urgent C-section, there were no medical facilities available in the camp. Fortunately, Ruqayya and her baby both survived, but many pregnant women in displacement camps in Syria lack access to prenatal care, postpartum services, and newborn care. In these circumstances, it's not surprising to find a greater percentage of women dying from pregnancy-related causes.

Some of the other countries you might find yourself in with high levels of gender inequality include Afghanistan, Chad, Côte d'Ivoire, Mali, Niger, and Yemen. These countries have much worse maternal mortality rates than Syria does; in Chad, for instance, women die in 856 out of every 100,000 live births. The rate of teenage pregnancies in Syria is also fairly low; 39 out of every 1,000 women between the ages of fifteen and nineteen give birth. But even in a country with a low teenage pregnancy rate, the average age at which women marry and have their first child can be low. Reports suggest that, in Syria, one response to the violence has been to force more girls into marriage before the age of eighteen. This matters because, across the globe, when women have children at younger ages, it decreases their likelihood of getting more education and, therefore, of having a paid job, especially a decent paid job. Thus, it makes gender equality harder to achieve. Like Ruqayya, you'll find being pregnant much more hazardous to your health. You'll be less likely to get secondary education (schooling past the primary or elementary level); 35 percent of women in Syria have achieved at least some secondary education, compared to 43 percent of men. You'll work, but your work will probably not be in the formal labor market, and you're therefore less likely to be paid or paid well. Only 12 percent of women in your country are working for pay, compared to 71 percent of men.

These inequalities in education and job market participation also mean less gender equality in positions of power. As far as measures of political participation go, only 12 percent of the seats in the Syrian parliament are occupied by women.

Gender inequality will be important to your experience of gender. So will gender socialization. Gender socialization is the process of learning how to fit into the particular gender to which you've been assigned. Who does that socializing is important, so you need to know who's going to spend most of her or his time taking care of you. You need to know who your primary caregiver is going to be.

↗ Your primary caregiver is a woman. **GO TO 34.**

↖ Your primary caregiver is a man. **GO TO 35.**

↘ Your primary caregiver is a group of people. **GO TO 26.**

57

You're born in the United States, a country with medium levels of gender inequality. According to the UN's most current Gender Inequality Index, your country ranks 43 out of 188 countries, while on the Global Gender Gap Index, you're 49 out of 144.

In the United States, you have one of the worst rates of women dying from pregnancy-related complications in the developed world. For every 100,000 live births in the United States, 14 women die of pregnancy-related causes. Unlike other countries in the developed world, the maternal mortality rate in your country is rising, rather than declining. As a mother in the United States, you're three times as likely as your Canadian neighbors and six times as likely as Scandinavian women to die during the maternal period (the time between the start of your pregnancy and one year after the delivery of your baby or termination of the pregnancy). If you're African American, low-income, or live in a rural area, your chances of dying from pregnancy-related causes increase. But women of all races and income levels, living in diverse geographical areas, are vulnerable. There are lots of factors that explain why it's increasingly dangerous for you to give birth in the United States, including uneven access to health care, as well as government funding being directed away from maternal care.

Even with the record number of women elected to Congress in 2018 (including the first Native American women and first Muslim American women ever to be elected), your country still isn't doing as well as other countries in women's representation in the government. As far as measures of empowerment go, only 22 percent of the seats in the United States legislature are occupied by women. The United States ranks ninety-ninth globally in terms of the percentage of women in the legislature, which puts you roughly in the middle. As of this writing, there are 23 women in the Senate (out of 100 total senators) and more than 100* are projected to win a seat in the House of Representatives (out of 435 total representatives).

Some of the other countries with medium levels of gender inequality include Hungary, Latvia, Malaysia, Malta, Mongolia, Slovakia, and the United Arab Emirates. Some of these are developing countries, like Malaysia, and others are developed countries, like Hungary.

---

*This book was written during the 2018 midterm elections, where a record number of women were elected, but some elections were not finalized before the printing of this book. Karma Allen, "More than 100 Women Elected to Congress in Historic Midterms," ABC News, November 7, 2018, https://abcnews.go.com/Politics/100-women-elected-us-house-historic-election/story?id=59019553.

In a country like the United States, levels of gender inequality aren't as bad as they could be. You're much more likely as a girl to receive an education and be paid for your work. Women are doing slightly better than men in the area of education, with 95.4 percent of women achieving at least some secondary education (schooling past the primary or elementary level), compared to 95.1 percent of men. You've also achieved high levels of equality in terms of economic status, as 56 percent of women in your country are working for pay, compared to 68 percent of men. But your government still doesn't come close to equal representation of women, and it can still be dangerous to give birth.

Gender inequality will be important to your experience of gender. So will gender socialization. Gender socialization is the process of learning how to fit into the particular gender to which you've been assigned. Who does that socializing is important, so you need to know who's going to spend most of her or his time taking care of you. You need to know who your primary caregiver is going to be.

↗ Your primary caregiver is a woman. **GO TO 34.**

↖ Your primary caregiver is a man. **GO TO 35.**

↘ Your primary caregiver is a group of people. **GO TO 26.**

58

You're born in Rwanda, a country with low gender inequality. Your country is currently ranked 4 out of 144 countries on the Global Gender Gap Index, with only Iceland, Norway, and Finland ahead of you. Your ranking according to the UN's most current Gender Inequality Index is worse, at 84 out of 188 countries.

Based on the UN's criteria, Rwanda has more gender inequality overall than the United States does. But in certain areas, Rwanda is actually doing better than the United States. The level of women's political empowerment in your country is pretty impressive. Looking just at the percentage of women in political power, your country ranks number one globally, with more than half (58 percent) of seats in your parliament held by women.

Your ranking on the UN index probably has to do with your maternal mortality ratio; for every 100,000 live births in Rwanda, 290 women die of pregnancy-related causes. Educational attainment is also very low in Rwanda, for both women and men—just 11 percent of women and 16 percent of men have received some secondary education (schooling past the primary or elementary level).

Rwanda is a developing country. More than that, it's a country still recovering from one of the twentieth century's most devastating genocides. In 1994, Hutu extremists led a mass slaughter resulting in the murder of 800,000 Tutsi adults and children over the course of 100 days. Although both women and men were killed in the genocide, many more men were imprisoned or fled the country, so that after the genocide, Rwanda was left with a population that was 70 percent women. Many of the jobs that had previously been occupied by men now had to be done by women out of necessity. Women in Rwanda have surpassed men in their labor market participation; 86 percent of women in your country are working for pay, compared to 83 percent of men. Women in your country stepped into the gap left by men across a wide range of occupations, not because they necessarily wanted equality for women, but because it was what they had to do in order to save their country.

In the aftermath of the genocide, women in your country banded together and demanded more power. They changed the Rwandan constitution to require that women hold at least 30 percent of all top political positions in the government. They changed marriage laws, giving women the right to inherit land, share marital assets, and establish credit on their own.

Women like you began delaying marriage in order to pursue education and a career.

These changes to gender inequality in Rwanda happened fast—over the course of about twenty years. So while your country has made big improvements in these large-scale measures of gender equality, other aspects of thinking about gender haven't quite caught up. Domestic violence is still common in your country and is widely accepted, as is demonstrated by a Rwandan saying, *niko zubakwa*, or "that's how marriages are built." One researcher found that even women who held some of the highest positions of power in the Rwandan government were still subservient to their husbands inside their homes. One of her research subjects, a woman who had been elected to the Rwandan parliament, still polished her husband's shoes and ironed his clothes. Her husband insisted that these tasks had to be done by his wife, rather than a housekeeper. Women like this, while they advocate for gender equality within their government positions, still feel fairly powerless to demand more equality in their own marriages and households.

So although your country has achieved incredible progress in regard to gender inequality, the fight is hardly over. Even when women gain power in institutions like the government, the economy, and education, it doesn't guarantee that areas like marriage and family will follow suit.

Gender inequality will be important to your experience of

gender. So will gender socialization. Gender socialization is the process of learning how to fit into the particular gender to which you've been assigned. Who does that socializing is important, so you need to know who's going to spend most of her or his time taking care of you. You need to know who your primary caregiver is going to be.

- ↗ Your primary caregiver is a woman. **GO TO 34.**
- ↖ Your primary caregiver is a man. **GO TO 35.**
- ↘ Your primary caregiver is a group of people. **GO TO 26.**

59

Learning to be a girl is different depending on where and when you are. But when gender socialization works well, it's easy to forget that the way gender works in your culture isn't the same as it works everywhere. If you master your own particular version of gender, it can seem as though this must be the right—and only—way for gender to be. The assumptions that people make about gender in other places may seem pretty weird.

If you're a little girl growing up in the contemporary United States, the rules for what is and isn't feminine might be a little looser than if you're a little boy. You're definitely expected to be passive and nurturing. So you're likely to be rewarded for cradling a baby doll or taking care of your younger siblings. The rewards can be obvious, like your parents telling you that you're a good girl when you play with the baby doll, or less obvious, like your parents simply smiling when you pretend the doll is your baby. When you do things that aren't considered correct for your gender, you're likely to be punished, but that punishment can be very subtle. If you get muddy investigating all the interesting things that live under rocks, your parents might scold you for ruining your shoes and your pretty dress. If you run around, can't sit still, and talk loudly, your parents and others might caution you to act more "ladylike."

Being boisterous and active is one example of a gender-typed behavior, or a behavior that will get rewarded or punished depending on the gender of the person who's engaging in the behavior. Giving other kids orders and taking the lead is another example of what it means to say a behavior is gender-typed. If a little boy orders other kids around, his parents, teachers, and other adults might be more likely to praise him. They might say, "Look at that future leader." Maybe they imagine him as a powerful politician. When a little girl does the same thing, the people around her respond to the behavior differently, by labeling her bossy. Being "bossy" implies that, as a little girl, you're taking authority that you don't really have. So when you get called bossy, you're learning that little girls aren't supposed to be confident or authoritative.

> **GENDER-TYPED BEHAVIOR**
>
> *n.* /ˈjen-dər ˈtīpt bi-ˈhā-vyər/
>
> Behavior that is rewarded or punished depending on the gender of the person engaging in the behavior.

We know that your parents and other people will start rewarding and punishing your behavior based on gender very early. Even as a baby, your parents are more likely to comfort you, as their daughter, when you cry than they are to comfort a son. The adults in your life will speak more conversationally to you than they would if you were a boy, to whom they'd be more likely to give instructions. When they tell you family stories, they'll emphasize emotions, while the stories they tell to boys will emphasize independence. Your parents and others will be less likely to engage in aggressive and challenging styles of play with you. And they'll give you different household chores compared to boys.

Just because you were assigned a girl and socialized as a girl doesn't mean that you'll necessarily end up feeling like a girl on the inside. Gender as a system is set up with the assumption that your gender assignment and your gender identity should match. In other words, your gender identity, or the way you feel about who you are, is supposed to be the same as the gender you were told you are at birth, or your gender assignment. That's how gender is supposed to work, but that doesn't mean that it's the best way or even that it works all the time.

↗ Your gender assignment and your gender identity match up. **GO TO 73.**

↘ Your gender assignment and your gender identity don't match. **GO TO 74.**

60

You're African American and your gender identity, gender assignment, and gender expression all line up. That means that you feel like a boy on the inside, you're labeled a boy, and you act like a boy.

As an African American boy, your experience of masculinity, even as a child, will be different from how boys of other racial backgrounds experience their gender. Your gender expression will be interpreted differently because of your race. In general, men tend to move through the world in ways that take up more space. "Manspreading," you might have heard it called. But as an African American man or boy, there might be a real danger in taking up space in the same way that white men and boys do. Research tells us that the deeply gendered logic used to excuse the behavior of white boys probably won't be applied to you, as an African American boy. Teachers and other authority figures will be less likely to excuse your rambunctious behavior with the expression, "Boys will be boys." Even from an early age, you'll be perceived as more sexual and aggressive than boys from other racial backgrounds. And because of all these beliefs about you, you're much more likely to be punished for a wide range of behaviors that are excused in white boys. At the very worst end of this spectrum of prejudicial treatment, you're much more likely to become the victim of police violence, as in the cases of twelve-year-old Tamir Rice, eighteen-year-old Michael Brown, fifteen-year-old Jordan Edwards, and so many others.

As an African American boy, it'll be more difficult for you to cash in on the patriarchal dividend of your society, or the rewards for being a boy and obeying all the rules for how boys are supposed to act. The truth is that even when you follow those rules, you're less likely to be rewarded.

↖ **GO TO 40.**

61

Your gender identity and your gender assignment match up, but your gender expression is different. You're a boy, but you like pink and purple instead of blue. You don't like playing sports or crashing into things. You don't walk with your feet splayed out to the side with lots of space between your legs like the other boys. You don't spread your arms and legs out to take up as much space as possible. You smile all the time (boys aren't really supposed to smile) and your voice is high. Just because you get labeled a boy and feel like a boy inside doesn't mean that you want to do all the things that boys are supposed to want to do.

Because you don't follow all the rules laid out for boys, you might be called a sissy or a wimp. If you live in an androcentric society, it's not okay as a boy to do feminine things. That's because androcentrism says that men and masculinity are better than women and femininity. If you're a boy doing feminine things, you're moving down the ladder instead of up. You're likely to get made fun of and be left out. Or worse.

You might be called gay or a fag. In many societies, gender and sexuality are presumed to be tied together. If you act feminine, people might assume that it reveals something about your sexuality—namely, that you're more likely to be attracted to other boys. Which is all a little weird if you think about it. Even with very young boys, people might assume that a boy who acts feminine—who plays with dolls or paints his nails or wears dresses—is revealing his sexuality. In reality, using nail polish doesn't have anything to do with who you want to have sex with or get married to, especially not when you're four years old.

The penalties for being a boy whose gender expression isn't masculine enough are generally greater than those for girls who aren't seen as feminine enough. Maybe that's because masculinity as a gender identity is more fragile than femininity—masculinity is an identity that has to be proven over and over again over the course of your life. Maybe it's because, as a boy, you're at the top of the gender hierarchy, so your behaviors are more tightly patrolled.

Maybe your gender expression as a boy is just a little bit off. You're a snazzy dresser and care about your clothes, but the clothes you wear are still easily perceived as "men's" clothes. But what if you don't like men's clothes? What if, all in all, you'd rather wear a skirt or a dress?

↗ You aren't interested in women's clothes. **GO TO 40.**

↘ You really like wearing clothes that aren't seen as appropriate for boys. **GO TO 45.**

↑ ↗

62

You tell your parents that your sense of who you are doesn't match up with what everyone else thinks. "I'm not really a girl, I'm a boy," you might say to them. Or maybe you feel like you're a very different kind of girl. Or even something completely different from either boy or girl.

You tell your parents or other family members, but they refuse to listen to you. Or they tell you that you're wrong. Maybe they ignore you altogether. They make you feel bad or weird or crazy. Or even worse, they yell at you or hit you. Some families kick their transgender kids out of the house. Why?

For some people, gender matters a lot. It is a system that they're deeply invested in, and a set of rules that they believe everyone should follow, including children like you. Among those rules is the idea that you are the gender you're born and that's that. You don't get to change, no matter how bad or wrong it feels to you. They might be scared about what could happen if those rules changed. If you could change your gender, what would that mean for their own sense of who they are?

Your parents might be afraid of what will happen to you

if you go from being a girl to a boy. They might be sad about losing a daughter, even if they'll be gaining a son. They might feel guilty, as if your gender-expansive or transgender identity is the result of something they did wrong as parents. They might find it hard to deal with the uncertainty of your gender-expansive identity. Maybe you know at once that you are a boy instead of a girl, but there might also be a period when you're figuring things out. It might be difficult for your parents to live through not knowing what your gender will be.

As a transgender kid, your power to assert your own identity is limited by the circumstances you find yourself in. If your parents don't support or even acknowledge your identity, it's hard to take action. If you find yourself in a family like this, you might struggle in school. Transgender kids who lack support are more likely to engage in self-harming activities and have higher rates of suicide. If you're lucky, maybe you'll find support in an online community or with a group of friends. You might stay in the closet, hiding your transgender identity until you can find a safer, more supportive environment.

⬉ For now, you conceal your transgender identity and live as a cisgender person. **GO TO 39.**

63

If you're a boy or a man who discovers that you really like wearing women's clothes, you might be a cross-dresser. That's different from being a transgender person. Your gender identity and gender assignment are still masculine. You feel like a man. You just feel like a man who likes wearing women's clothes. Maybe you consider it a way to embrace your feminine side. Maybe you only wear women's clothes in the privacy of your own home. Your cross-dressing might not be anything more elaborate than putting on a pair of women's underwear or a touch of makeup. Or you might like to go out in public fully dressed as a woman.

Being a cross-dresser doesn't imply anything about your sexual identity. You may be straight or gay or bisexual. Your cross-dressing might make you feel sexy, but it isn't necessarily something you do as part of the sex you have with partners. Your cross-dressing could start at a very early age or much later in life.

↖ **GO TO 40.**

↙ →

64

To be a drag queen is about more than just wearing women's clothes. Drag is a performance, a creative expression. Many drag queens describe it as an art form. It's a way of turning gender into something exciting and fun.

As a drag queen, you may or may not be gay. Many, but not all, drag queens are gay men. You might also be transgender, but you don't have to be in order to engage in drag. You'll probably have a drag name and persona, in addition to a street name and persona. You might get paid to perform drag, but not all drag queens are paid. The particular version of femininity that you perform might be greatly exaggerated or more low-key. When you're in drag, you might achieve social femaleness—that is, people might assume that you're a woman. Or you might not.

Some people who study drag argue that it exposes the true nature of gender. All of us, to some extent, are performing drag, and this is true regardless of our underlying biology or gender identity. We are all trying to create some coherent image of a certain gender, even though the idea of gender itself is something that we made up.

↗ You're a cisgender boy. **GO TO 40.**

↘ You're gender expansive. **GO TO 49.**

65

Courtship is the general term used to describe how people come together romantically and sexually. Sometimes courtship leads to marriage and sometimes it doesn't. What courtship looks like can vary a lot depending on where and who you are.

You're probably going to have a harder time finding that special someone if you're gay, lesbian, bisexual, transgender, genderqueer, or asexual. Because most societies are built on the assumption that everyone is cisgender and straight (which is to say, most societies are heteronormative and cisnormative), it's harder for you to find someone to love, have sex with, or marry. This is partly because there are fewer people available for you to date, so you're in a smaller potential dating pool.

Why are there fewer LGBTQ+ people out there for you to date? One reason is that if you live in a heteronormative culture, you're subject to compulsory heterosexuality. This is the idea that society puts a great deal of pressure on people to be straight. Compulsory heterosexuality makes it harder to come out if you are LGBTQ+, which makes it much harder for you to find other people who might be interested in dating you. In a society without compulsory heterosexuality, people wouldn't feel stigmatized for not being straight, which would make dating much easier.

But it's also true that because the society you're living in is probably heteronormative and cisnormative, you'll have to be careful about pursuing potential partners. In many times and places, being LGBTQ+ has been or is still seen as immoral or deviant, so trying to approach someone romantically has often been a very dangerous activity. It was only as recently as 2003 in the United States that all laws making homosexual behavior illegal were ruled unconstitutional. Up until that point, some states still had laws that would allow for the prosecution of people caught engaging in same-gender sexual behavior. Today, homosexual relationships are illegal in seventy-four countries. There are thirteen countries in which being homosexual is still punishable by death. Across the globe, violence against LGBTQ+ individuals persists, as in the 2017 mass shooting at a gay nightclub in Orlando, Florida, which resulted in 49 deaths. In some places, you might find yourself putting your life on the line in pursuit of love and intimacy. This is part of the reason why gay and lesbian subcultures have been

> **COMPULSORY HETEROSEXUALITY**
>
> *n.* /kəm-ˈpəls-rē
> ˌhe-tə-rō-ˌsek-shə-ˈwa-lə-tē/
>
> The pressure from society on individuals to be straight.

so important in the past and continue to be important today. People in the LGBTQ+ community need spaces, like gay bars, where they can safely find each other.

Most recently, online dating sites are making dating and courtship somewhat easier. These sites allow even LGBTQ+ people who are in relatively isolated locations to find each other.

↗ You get married. **GO TO 104.**

↘ You don't get married. **GO TO 105.**

66

Before you have surgery, your doctor will probably suggest that you start with hormone therapy. If you're in the United States, you'll have to receive a medical diagnosis of gender dysphoria before you'll be allowed to have surgery. Gender dysphoria refers specifically to the distress that results from the mismatch between your gender assignment and your gender identity. In the twentieth century, being transgender was considered a mental disorder that was known as gender-identity disorder. It wasn't until 2012 that diagnostic guidelines were changed to gender dysphoria. Today, medical professionals focus on the psychological and emotional distress that results from how people react to your transgender identity—rather than treating your identity itself as an illness.

> **GENDER DYSPHORIA**
>
> *n.* /ˈjendər disˈfôr-ē-ə/
>
> The condition of feeling one's emotional and psychological identity as male or female to be opposite to a preassigned gender.

But because a medical diagnosis is still required for surgery in the United States, doctors, surgeons, and psychiatrists serve as gatekeepers, making decisions about who can have access to hormone therapy and surgical procedures. In the past, you'd probably be denied hormones or surgery if you were a woman who'd ever been pregnant or had a child. Doctors were also likely to turn down patients whose sexual identity didn't line up in the way that doctors felt that it should. For example, one trans man was denied treatment because he wanted to live as a gay man. Doctors could not comprehend how a woman could want to become a man and still be sexually attracted to men.

As a trans man undergoing hormone therapy, you'll probably be taking testosterone, and there are many changes that you can expect to see to your body. Your skin will become thicker and oilier. Many of the experiences of taking hormone therapy are like those of puberty. For instance, you might develop some acne. Your breasts will probably not change in size, but you might have some soreness. The fat in your body will shift away from your hips and thighs. You might see more fat develop around your belly and midsection. Your arms and legs will become more muscular. Your overall muscle mass may increase, depending on factors like diet and exercise.

The muscles of your vocal chords might thicken, resulting in a deeper voice. Just as this doesn't happen for all cisgender boys at puberty, it doesn't happen for all trans men with hormone therapy. But like cisgender boys going through puberty, your voice may scratch and break until it settles into a normal range.

Your hair will probably get thicker and grow faster. But how much and where your hair shows up still depends on genetics. If most of the men in your family have little facial hair, you probably won't have much facial hair, either. After all, not all cisgender men can grow a beard.

Your emotional state might change due to testosterone, just as it does for cisgender boys going through puberty. You might also experience a change in your sexual desire. Your clitoris will begin to grow and will become even larger when aroused. The way you experience orgasms may also change.

Your period may become lighter and shorter in duration before you eventually stop having a period altogether. While testosterone greatly reduces the chances of becoming pregnant, it's not impossible. If you want to become pregnant later, you might still be able to once you stop taking testosterone. However, taking testosterone for long periods of time will likely make it harder for you to conceive.

You may feel as a trans man that the bodily changes brought on by testosterone are enough to give you a body that you matches up with your gender identity and gender expression. But you might also realize that some sort of surgical intervention is what you need in order to get the body that feels right to you.

↗ You have gender-confirming surgery. **GO TO 86.**

↖ You don't have gender-confirming surgery and you live in a place where gender and sexuality are seen as connected. **GO TO 87.**

↘ You don't have gender-confirming surgery and you live in a place where gender and sexuality aren't seen as connected. **GO TO 88.**

67

You feel that surgery isn't for you, and that's okay. There are as many ways to be a trans man as there are to be a cisgender man. Maybe hormone therapy alone gives you the body that feels right for you. Maybe you don't pursue hormone therapy at all. You might be okay with dressing as a man, changing your name, and asking people to use masculine pronouns.

Because the dominant stories of the transgender experience focus on sex reassignment or gender-confirming surgery, you might find yourself having to explain your decision to other people, both within and outside of the transgender community. Because having gender-confirming surgery is seen as normal to the transgender experience, you might be questioned for not following that norm.

If you don't have surgery or take hormone therapy, you might find it more difficult to achieve social maleness. That means that you might have difficulty passing what some trans men describe as the "sir test." Do people who interact with you in your day-to-day life perceive you as a man and call you sir? If not, then your gender attribution might remain ambiguous to most people. Gender attribution is the gender that other people assign to you when they interact with you. We engage in gender attribution all the time, using a series of cues in order to help us figure out what a person's gender is. We pay attention to what a person looks like, but also to things like who they're with, how they interact, and how much power they have. We might also have access to textual cues—a driver's license or job application. Or we may use mythic cues—the stories we tell each other about gender. So, maybe if you see someone changing a baby's diaper, you assume that it's a woman, because your culture's stories tell you that a woman is much more likely to be changing a diaper than a man.

Our default when it comes to gender attribution is men. That is, because being a man is seen as the norm or the "right" gender to be in our society, we start by assuming that people are men and then look for cues that tell us otherwise. This works in your favor as a trans man. It might make it slightly easier for you to achieve social maleness without hormones or surgery.

↖ **GO TO 87.**

68

You're the first in your class or your group of friends to hit puberty. You develop breasts before all the rest of the girls. You start your period and hair starts growing in new places (in your armpits and between your legs). Being first seems like a good thing, doesn't it? Maybe.

The bodily changes that happen to girls at puberty are stressful enough by themselves. But there are also a lot of cultural meanings that get attached to these biological changes. Your culture might send you messages that your new body is something you should be ashamed of. Before you hit puberty, you might have been able to go without a shirt sometimes, like boys, but not anymore. You have to wear a bra. Maybe your parents and other family members celebrate your period, but they will probably also warn you about all the unpleasant implications of your new status. Men and boys will look at you in a different way now, your parents and other adults might tell you. You can get pregnant. If you were a tomboy, your family might suggest that you give up the boyish parts of your gender expression at puberty. No more acting like a boy. Many girls experience puberty as an entrance into a scarier world with a lot more rules. Hitting puberty early doesn't really help with all these negative implications. In fact, it might just make them worse.

Puberty is one part of how your experience of gender will be embodied, which means that gender as a category interacts with our bodies in important ways. One of those ways is through ability or disability. Gender intersects with the degree to which your body is seen as able—"normal" and capable of doing the things required of bodies in your society—and therefore incapable to some extent of doing the things expected of "normal" bodies.

↗ You have a temporarily abled body. **GO TO 93.**

↘ You have a disabled body. **GO TO 94.**

69

It seems like you're the last girl in the whole world to hit puberty! All the rest of the girls have breasts, and your chest is still disappointingly flat. Your period doesn't come, and all the parts of your body that are supposed to be growing hair are still bare. Being last sucks.

When puberty comes late, you might feel like you're stuck in place while everyone else is moving ahead. There are a lot of negative meanings that get attached to puberty for girls, but there are some things to feel positive about. You might really be looking forward to the grown-up feeling that comes from shaving your legs for the first time.

Around the time they hit puberty, many girls experience a big drop in self-esteem. Regardless of whether you hit puberty late or early, as a girl, you may find that your self-confidence decreases. You might not feel as good about your body as you did when you were younger. You may feel less optimistic about your future possibilities. Research suggests that this isn't biological, but partly a result of what your culture tells you about what it means to be a woman. While the process of becoming a man is seen as a good thing, entering into womanhood can feel scary instead of exciting.

Puberty is one part of how your experience of gender will be embodied, which means that gender as a category interacts with our bodies in important ways. One of those ways is through ability or disability. Gender intersects with the degree to which your body is seen as able—"normal" and capable of doing the things required of bodies in your society—and therefore incapable to some extent of doing the things expected of "normal" bodies.

↗ You have a temporarily abled body. **GO TO 93.**

↘ You have a disabled body. **GO TO 94.**

70

Though your gender may have been assigned as a girl or boy at birth, and you've lived your life up until this point assuming that gender assignment was correct, at puberty things don't go exactly as expected. You may be an intersex person. Some intersex conditions are apparent at birth, but others don't emerge until puberty. Perhaps you're a boy and you start to develop breasts and menstruate. Or you're a girl and you don't develop breasts or get your period. What happens now?

Your intersex condition is very unlikely to be dangerous or bad for your health. But your parents and doctors may still want to intervene to "fix" you. If you've been raised as a boy and doctors discover that you have ovaries, they might suggest surgery to remove them. You'd think that by the time you've reached this age, it would be too late for doctors and parents to try to conceal the facts of your condition from you. But, in fact, many doctors and parents choose to do just that, even when intersex conditions are discovered at puberty. One intersex woman was told that the series of surgeries she had was to prevent her from getting cancer, instead of to "treat" her intersex condition. It's not surprising, then, that many intersex people are relieved when they finally find out the real reason for surgeries and other medical treatments.

Your experience of puberty, which is already a stressful time for most people, will have an added layer of fear and uncertainty. Maybe your parents and doctors will be open with you about what's happening to your body, and you'll be allowed to participate in your own medical decisions. Maybe you'll come to some sense of how you want to live your gender going forward.

↗ You feel like a woman. **GO TO 50.**

↖ You feel like a man. **GO TO 87.**

↘ You feel like something else. **GO TO 18.**

71

When you were born, or at some other point along the way, you were assigned a masculine gender. You also feel like a boy inside. Your gender assignment and your gender identity match up, which means that you're cisgender. So what? What does it actually mean to feel like a boy or a man?

You're a boy, sure, but does that mean that you're never allowed to show any interest in things like clothes or makeup or the color pink? Maybe you really like pink. And you'd like to wear glittery barrettes in your hair and play with baby dolls. Maybe you cry a lot and never get over the fear of having a ball thrown at you very fast and very hard.

The truth is that even if you're cisgender, not every part of your gender identity will necessarily match up with your gender expression, or the way your culture tells you to perform your gender. As Kate Bornstein, a transgender activist, points out, at some point gender as a

> **GENDER EXPRESSION**
>
> *n.* /ˈjen-dər ik-ˈspre-shən/
>
> The aspects of one's behavior, mannerisms, and appearance that are associated with that gender in a particular cultural context.

system lets all of us down. At some point in your life, you will have a thought, have a feeling, or engage in some behavior that does not perfectly match the rules laid out for your gender. As a boy, the repercussions of a mismatch will vary depending on your racial background.

↗ Your gender identity, gender assignment, and gender expression all match up, and you're white. **GO TO 55.**

↖ Your gender identity, gender assignment, and gender expression all match up, and you're African American. **GO TO 60.**

↘ Your gender expression doesn't match up with your gender identity and gender assignment. **GO TO 61.**

72

When you were born, everyone assumed that you were a boy, but you suspect that everyone got it wrong. You don't feel like a boy, so your gender assignment and your gender identity don't match up. You might start telling people that you're not a boy when you're as young as two or three years old. You might tell your parents that you know you're not really a boy—that you don't want a penis and you prefer wearing dresses. You didn't get any say in the gender assignment that was given to you when you were born, and now you're letting everyone know that they might have gotten it wrong. If something about the gender you've been assigned doesn't feel right, you might be a gender-expansive or transgender person.

Transgender is the umbrella term that's generally used to describe when your gender identity doesn't match your gender assignment at birth. It can also refer more specifically to people whose gender identity is "opposite" or "across from" the gender they were assigned at birth. In your case, the opposite gender would be girl.

The term *gender expansive* includes those who are transgender, but also anyone who expands their own culture's commonly held expectations about gender, whether that means how they express their gender, how they identify, or the norms they choose to follow or not to follow. People with nonbinary identities would be an example of what it means to be gender expansive.

> **TRANSGENDER**
>
> *adj.* /ˈtranz-ˈjen-dər/
>
> Relating to or being a person whose gender identity differs from the gender the person was assigned at birth.

What happens to you as a transgender or gender-expansive kid depends a lot on how the people around you respond to you.

↗ Your parents reject your transgender or gender-expansive identity. **GO TO 28.**

↘ Your parents accept your transgender or gender-expansive identity. **GO TO 29.**

73

You were assigned a feminine gender when you were born, and you feel like a girl. You're cisgender, which means that your gender assignment and gender identity match up. But what exactly does it mean to say you feel like a girl?

Maybe you're a girl, but you really like looking at all the creepy-crawly things under rocks, even if you do get muddy. Maybe you like getting muddy. Does that make you feel less like a girl? What if you never cry? What if you hate baby dolls?

Gender identity is the way we feel inside, and "girl" is one label to put on those feelings. But the truth is that even if you're cisgender, not every part of your gender identity will necessarily match up with your gender expression, or the way your culture tells you to perform your gender. As Kate Bornstein, a transgender activist, points out, at some point gender as a system lets all of us down. At some point in your life, you will have a

> **CISGENDER**
>
> *adj.* /(ˌ)sis-ˈjen-dər/
>
> Relating to or being a person whose gender identity corresponds with the gender the person was assigned at birth.

thought, have a feeling, or engage in some behavior that does not perfectly match the rules laid out for your gender. Another way to say this is that your gender expression won't always line up with your gender assignment and your gender identity.

- ↗ Your gender identity, gender assignment, and gender expression all match up. **GO TO 43.**
- ↘ Your gender expression doesn't match up with your gender identity and gender assignment. **GO TO 44.**

74

You were assigned a feminine gender when you were born, but it doesn't feel right. You don't feel like a girl, and you might start telling people as soon as you can. At as young as two or three years old, some children let their parents know that there's something wrong about their gender. You might wonder why you have a girl's body when you know that you're really meant to be a boy. Gender assignment happened for you when you were too young to have a say in the matter, but now you're asserting your own, deeply felt sense of who you truly are. If something about the gender you've been assigned doesn't feel right, you might be a transgender or gender-expansive person.

Transgender is the umbrella term that's generally used to describe when your gender identity doesn't match your gender assignment at birth. It can also refer more specifically to people whose gender identity is "opposite" or "across from" the gender they were assigned at birth. In your case, the "opposite" gender would be boy.

The term *gender expansive* includes those who are trans-gender, but also anyone who expands their own culture's commonly held expectations about gender, whether that means how they express their gender, how they identify themselves, or the norms they choose to follow or not to follow. People with nonbinary identities would be an example of what it means to be gender expansive.

What happens to you as a transgender or gender-expansive kid depends a lot on how the people around you respond to you.

↗ Your parents reject your transgender or gender-expansive identity. **GO TO 62.**

↘ Your parents accept your transgender or gender-expansive identity. **GO TO 27.**

75

As a gay man, you might find that people expect you to live your gender in certain ways. That's because of all the complicated ways in which gender and sexuality intersect in your culture. You might be expected to care more about your appearance than straight men do. People might expect you to talk a certain way—with a lisp or in a more animated style. There might be certain sports and activities—like gymnastics, dance, or choir—that people assume that you're more likely to participate in. Maybe people assume that you know more about topics like musicals and fashion. In general, you'll be expected to be and act more feminine than straight men, but feminine in very specific ways. For instance, no one will expect you to be better at taking care of children just because you're a gay man. In fact, some people might feel that you shouldn't be around children because of your sexual identity. Even though the overwhelming majority of men who sexually abuse children are straight, people might still feel that it's dangerous to allow you access to kids.

If you don't conform to all these expectations, people will probably express surprise and maybe even say things like, "You don't act gay" or "You don't seem gay."

Chances are you'll find yourself in a society that's heteronormative, a place where being straight is assumed to be normal and right. Living in that kind of society will make a lot of things difficult for you, including finding someone to love.

> **HETERONORMATIVE**
>
> *adj.* / ˌhē-tə-rō-ˈnȯr-mə-tiv/
>
> Based on the attitude that hetero-sexuality is the only normal and natural expression of sexuality.

↖ **GO TO 65.**

76

You're a gender-expansive kid who doesn't feel like a woman or a man. That could mean that you also don't identify yourself as any of the categories for sexual identity that are dependent upon gender. For instance, if you really don't think of yourself as a woman, then you might argue that it makes no sense to think of yourself as a lesbian, either. After all, categories like lesbian, gay man, straight woman, straight man, bisexual woman, and bisexual man are all based on the assumption that everyone has some sort of gender that lines up with masculinity and femininity. If there is no such thing as gender, the categories for sexual identity become sort of obsolete.

So what do you do? Just because you don't identify as a man or a woman doesn't necessarily mean that you aren't interested in having sexual and romantic relationships.

Maybe you identify as pansexual. If you're pansexual, it means that your sexual and romantic desires aren't limited by categories of gender assignment, gender expression, or gender identity. Your attraction to someone isn't dependent upon the gender they were assigned at birth or on how they live their gender or on what they feel their gender is. None of that matters to you. Your sexual and romantic desires basically have nothing to do with gender.

If you're in a culture with a strong link between gender and sexuality, being pansexual might sound sort of weird. But you could argue that pansexuality makes more sense than all the other categories of sexual identity, which when you get down to it, can be pretty confusing. Say you're a straight woman. What is it exactly that you're attracted to? People with penises? Or people who were told they were boys when they were born? Or people who dress, act, and think in masculine ways? Or are you attracted to people who feel like they're men on the inside?

> **PANSEXUAL**
>
> *adj.* /ˌpan-ˈsek-sh(ə-)wəl/
>
> Being a person whose sexual desire or attraction is not limited to people of a particular gender identity or sexual orientation.

For the sake of argument, let's say that to be a straight woman means that you're attracted to people with penises. That would include trans men who've had gender-confirming surgery that included the construction of a penis. It also assumes that the fact that someone has a penis provides you with important information about your sexual and romantic compatibility. Does it, though? If one of your nonnegotiable requirements for a partner is that they can make you laugh, does having a penis have anything to do with that?

If you don't identify as a woman or a man and aren't using gender as a criterion for finding your soul mate, maybe you're actually ahead of the game.

↖   **GO TO 65.**

77

As a lesbian woman, you might find that people expect you to live your gender in certain ways. That's because of all the complicated ways in which gender and sexuality intersect in your culture. You might find that people expect you to dress like a man and wear your hair short. They might be surprised if you wear lipstick or frilly skirts. There might be certain sports—like softball—that people assume you're more likely to participate in. Maybe they'll assume that you are a feminist or that you hate men. Generally, people will expect you to act more masculine than straight women do, and they might be surprised when you don't.

Your lesbian identity doesn't really affect how you express your gender, but in a culture like this, people will believe that it does. The power of those beliefs along with the strength of heteronormativity—the assumption that being straight is right and normal—will lead some people to make weird assumptions about your relationships with women. They might ask questions like, "Who's the man?"—implying that even in a relationship between two women, someone has to be masculine and someone has to be feminine.

Your experience of being a lesbian woman will vary depending on other identities that intersect with your gender and sexual identity. Being a lesbian isn't necessarily harder or easier if you belong to one racial or ethnic group compared to others. But it's also true that when many people picture "lesbian" in their head, that image is more likely to be a white woman than a person of color. That's because white is generally the default in American society, and that extends to categories of sexual identity as well. Those perceptions, along with the particular history and culture of your racial or ethnic group, can shape what it means for you to be a lesbian. For example, when Arab American lesbians come out to family and friends, they are often told that there is no such thing as an Arab American lesbian.

↗ You're an Arab American lesbian. **GO TO 121.**

↘ You're not an Arab American lesbian. **GO TO 65.**

78

Already the path of your gender adventure is turning out to be fairly complicated, full of unexpected twists and turns. We could pretend that gender is the only or the most important thing that determines where you end up along the path of your life. But that's not really how it works. We are all touched by gender, but also by other aspects of who we are, like our racial and ethnic backgrounds. Your race and ethnicity have a lot to do with what your gender path looks like and your experiences along the way.

Your gender and your race probably intersect in your daily life, and that's basically what an intersectional approach to gender means. It's impossible to separate out what parts of your experiences have to do with your racial or ethnic background and what parts have to do with your gender. You move through life as both.

One way to think about an intersectional approach is to always ask yourself the question, "Which people?" If someone tells you that boys underperform in school, you should ask yourself, *Which boys?* or *Which girls? White boys? Asian American girls? Middle-class boys or working-class boys?* Questions like these make us think about the fact that the experiences of all people of the same gender aren't the same. Nor are the experience of all people of the same racial or ethnic background.

Your racial or ethnic background will probably be an important part of how you experience your gender, but we can't predict exactly how; however, there are some things that might be true.

↗ You're an African American man. **GO TO 132.**

↖ You're an African American woman. **GO TO 133.**

↖ You're a Latinx woman. **GO TO 134.**

→ You're a Latinx man. **GO TO 135.**

↖ You're an Asian American man. **GO TO 136.**

↖ You're an Asian American woman. **GO TO 137.**

↘ You're an Arab American man. **GO TO 138.**

→ You're an Arab American woman. **GO TO 139.**

↖ You're a white man. **GO TO 140.**

↘ You're a white woman. **GO TO 141.**

79

You're a straight man, but that doesn't mean that there aren't implications for you of living in a society where gender and sexuality are connected. Because of the complex ways that gender and sexuality intersect, there are certain expectations that people think you should meet. People might expect you, as a straight man, not to put too much effort into your appearance. When there's music playing, no one will be surprised if you don't dance. Other men might try to get you to brag about having sex with women or to talk about women's bodies with them. You might even be expected to engage in street harassment—yelling at women as they walk by on the street or in other public settings. People might assume that you enjoy pornography. If there's a jar that needs to be opened or something heavy that needs to be lifted, you're likely to be the one people will ask for help. There might be certain sports and activities—like football, fixing cars, or hunting—that people assume that you're more likely to participate in.

Because of the way that gender and sexuality are connected in your society, you'll face the constant danger of being called gay or a fag. By and large, when you're called these things, it won't have anything to do with who you love or who you want to have sex with. These terms are used to patrol your masculinity, not your sexuality. High school boys call each other fag for a wide range of things that have nothing to do with sex or love—for tripping in the hallway or wearing the wrong clothes. As a straight man, society is set up to meet your needs, but you have to walk a very narrow line in order to fully benefit from the system.

The good news is that because you're in a heteronormative society, you're in a place where being straight like you is seen as normal and right. That will make the process of finding someone to love significantly easier than it is for people who aren't straight like you.

↖ **GO TO 101.**

80

In a culture where gender and sexuality are closely connected, there will be a set of expectations about how you're supposed to be, even as a straight woman. Most of them will have nothing to do with who you want to love. As a straight woman, people might expect you to care a lot about the clothes you wear and how you look in general. They might expect you to have long hair and to wear makeup. If you get married, people might assume that you've been planning your wedding since you were a little girl. There might be certain sports and activities—like cheerleading, babysitting, or shopping—that people assume that you're more likely to participate in.

As a straight woman, sexual scripts will tell you that you're supposed to be the passive partner in sexual interactions. A sexual script is a norm that tells us how to feel, act, and think about sex. For straight women, the sexual script says that you might have to be persuaded to have sex. Your culture tells you that you're supposed to walk a very fine line between being sexually experienced—which is okay—and too sexually experienced—which is definitely not okay. It's more accepted now than it was in the past for you to have sex without being married, but you're still likely to be labeled a "slut" if you have too much sex. The men you have sex with probably won't be labeled the same way, no matter how many people they have sex with, and that's a good example of the double standard. The double standard dictates that certain behaviors, often sexual behaviors, that are seen as okay for men are punished and stigmatized when women engage in them.

This sexual script about feminine sexual passivity might make your sexual and intimate relationships with men complicated. Though consent is an issue for everyone engaging in sexual activity, it becomes especially problematic with straight men and women, both of whom have grown up with messages telling them that women have to be persuaded and coerced into having sex.

The good news is that because you're a straight woman in a heteronormative society—a place where being straight like you is seen as right and normal—finding someone to love will be much easier for you than it is for your lesbian counterparts.

↖ **GO TO 101.**

81

In a society where gender and sexuality are strongly connected, even categories like bisexuality are still defined in relation to gender. Someone who is bisexual is sexually and romantically attracted to people of both genders. Though there are some expectations that go along with being bisexual, this identity is fuzzier as a social role, so there are fewer expectations attached to being bisexual than there are to being gay or straight. Still, some people might think that as a bisexual man, you're really just undecided. That is, they might assume that you're really gay or that you're really straight. Categories of sexual identity are structured to be discrete, which means that you have to be either one or the other. Being bisexual flies in the face of the assumption that, deep down, everyone is either gay or straight. People might treat your bisexual identity as something that you'll eventually grow out of. They'll see it as a temporary state.

> **BISEXUAL**
>
> *adj.* /(ˌ)bī-ˈsek-sh(ə-)wəl/
>
> Being a person who is romantically and sexually attracted to males and females.

Because you're in a heteronormative society—one in which being straight is seen as normal and right—you're likely to find the experience of dating a bit more complicated.

↖ **GO TO 65.**

82

As a bisexual woman, you're sexually and romantically attracted to both men and women, but your gender will still matter to how you experience your sexuality. Because you're a bisexual woman, people might assume that you're more promiscuous, or that you have sex with a lot of people. Some might think that because you don't limit yourself to being attracted to just men or just women, your life is somehow a sexual free-for-all. People might ask you, "Are you attracted to everyone?"—which is a pretty stupid question to ask. People who are attracted just to other women aren't attracted to *all* women, and people who are attracted only to men aren't attracted to *all* men. If you're bisexual, why should you be attracted to all men and all women?

You'd think that being attracted to both women and men might make dating easier for you. But in a society that's set up based on the assumption that everyone is straight and that's the way it should be, dating might still get complicated.

↖ **GO TO 65.**

↑ ↗

83

To be asexual means that you're not interested in having a sexual relationship with anyone. This identity is a fairly recent addition to the existing categories of sexuality. As with other sexual identities, asexual people often have to fight for their identities to not be treated like a disease or a disorder. Many people will assume that you have some sort of sexual dysfunction (you don't) or that you just haven't met the right person yet (also not true). Other people will insist that everyone has to be interested in sex because it's part of human nature, but there's no evidence that this is true. You might get incorrectly lumped together with celibate people, but being asexual is not the same as being celibate. Celibate people, like priests and nuns, choose to give up sexual activity. Being asexual isn't a choice; it's part of who you are.

ASEXUAL

adj. /(ˌ)ā-ˈsek-sh(ə-)wəl/

Being a person who is not interested in having a sexual relationship or who does not experience sexual desire toward others.

Being asexual doesn't necessarily mean that you're not interested in having a romantic relationship with someone.

- ↗ You are interested in having a romantic relationship with someone. **GO TO 102.**
- ↘ You are not interested in having a romantic relationship with someone. **GO TO 103.**

84

You're demisexual, a relatively new category of sexual identity. As someone who's demisexual, you need to feel a strong emotional connection with someone before you experience any sexual attraction. All your friends who go on about having crushes on celebrities or that barista in the coffee shop or someone they've never even had a conversation with? That's not for you, and you probably don't quite get it when your friends talk about feeling attracted to people they don't really know.

As a demisexual person, you experience sexual desire. You might masturbate and have sexual fantasies. But you're not interested in engaging in sexual activity unless you really know someone. Because of this lack of interest in sex outside of emotional connection, being demisexual is sometimes seen as a subcategory of asexuality. The "demi-" prefix

> **DEMISEXUAL**
>
> *adj.* /ˈde-mē-ˈsek-sh(ə-)wəl/
>
> Being a person who does not experience sexual attraction to another unless one experiences a strong emotional connection with that person first.

communicates the idea that this identity is halfway between being sexual and asexual.

As with asexual identity, you can be demisexual and sexually attracted to people across the gender spectrum. What's most important to you, though, is first having a deep, emotional connection with your partner.

↖ **GO TO 65.**

↑   ↗

85

Your identity is *queer*, a term that has a long and interesting history. In its current definition, *queer* is an umbrella term for sexual and gender minorities who are not heterosexual and/or cisgender. So your identification as queer could be based on your sexual identity or your gender identity or some combination of the two.

If you look up *queer* in an older dictionary, the first definition you might find is an adjective describing something strange or peculiar. Your grandparents or other older folks you know might still use *queer* this way, to describe things that seem weird to them but have nothing to do with sexuality. "This is queer

---

QUEER

adj. /ˈkwir/

Describing people who are not heterosexual and/or cisgender.

---

weather we're having today," they might say, and by that, they do not mean that the weather is homosexual or transgender.

Sometime in the late nineteenth century, people began using *queer* as a derogatory term for gay and lesbian people. This slur still drew on the original meaning—to call someone queer was to say that they were abnormal because of their sexual identity. But this version of *queer* is definitely an insult, and some people still use it this way.

But in the 1990s, queer theory was born, and this brought about another transformation in the meaning of the word. Queer theory is a perspective that brings together elements from feminism, the gay and lesbian rights movement, and a more general movement in philosophy and other disciplines that questions the nature of truth. At the intersection of all these different trends, queer theory is an approach that is very skeptical of categories—including categories like woman, man, lesbian, and gay. Categories, queer theory argues, will always exclude some people, because in order to create a category, you have to have a set of criteria for who fits and who doesn't. And once you have a set of criteria, there will be people who get left out. For example, the feminist movement was organized around the category of "women." But how do we decide who are and aren't women? If you use an essentialist definition and say that women are those who are born with a vagina or XX chromosomes, then you've already excluded many intersex people as well as trans women. Queer theory argues that this aspect of categories is kind of, well, crappy. Creating categories is connected to power—the ability to say one person is on the inside of this category while another is on the outside.

If categories can be used to exclude people, then maybe the best thing to do would be to get rid of the categories altogether. Or if that's not possible, we should at least acknowledge that categories are something that we should be a bit suspicious about. Instead of calling ourselves lesbian or gay or women or men, what if we just called ourselves queer? We're queer in the sense that, yes, we are strange and weird, and that's okay. In fact, it's better than okay. It's awesome. Queer theory draws on this first meaning of the word because part of the mission of queer theory is to reveal the weirdness of categories and other ways of thinking about gender and sexuality. Queer theory encourages us to embrace the weirdness. And using the term *queer* specifically takes a word that was a slur and turns it into something positive, which can be a very powerful thing. Identifying as queer has the potential to transform the word from an insult hurled at people to an identity to feel good about.

Identifying yourself as queer, then, could signal that you're wary of existing categories. It can also mean that you want to signal your alliance with all people who are marginalized on the basis of gender and sexuality, or by existing categories. In this broadest application of the term *queer*, you're expressing your alliance with, well, everyone. All of us are in some ways marginalized by existing categories, because none of us fit them perfectly all the time. So for some, but not all, queer theorists, all of us are really queer, in this way of looking at it.

Generally, though, if you identify as queer, it probably means that you're in a category that's marginalized in some way due to gender or sexuality.

↖ **GO TO 65.**

86

Sex-reassignment (or gender-confirming) surgery usually will happen only after hormone therapy. If your doctor or medical professional follows the World Professional Association for Transgender Health (WPATH) standard of care, you'll have to live for a year as a man before you're able to have gender-confirming surgery. This is often called the Real-Life Test, because it's a test of whether you can successfully go through all aspects of your daily life—including public aspects like going to school, maintaining employment, or volunteering in the community—as a man.

Once you've cleared that hurdle, you can have gender-confirming surgery. In this procedure, your uterus and ovaries will be removed. You can also have a penis constructed for you using tissue from your forearm or other parts of your body that allow for physical sensation. A more difficult procedure extends your urethra to allow you to pee while standing up. This is done because the urethra you were born with is shorter than the urethra of a cisgender man. In general, the surgical procedures for creating a penis are more difficult than the surgical procedures that trans women undergo—and as such, many trans men forgo this option.

The surgical procedures involving the removal of your reproductive organs and the construction of a penis are often called bottom surgery. You might also elect to have top surgery, which would mean the surgical removal of your breasts. Or you might have top surgery without any alteration to your reproductive organs or construction of a penis. In fact, some trans men keep their reproductive organs so that they can still become pregnant and give birth.

↖ **GO TO 87.**

87

If you're in a European-influenced culture after the nineteenth century, gender and sexuality are understood to be deeply connected. This is especially true for men. In the nineteenth century, people began to study sexuality scientifically for the first time, but what they mostly studied was the behavior of men.

For a period in the nineteenth century, male homosexuality wasn't seen as connected to being less masculine, but instead as a natural result of masculinity. Basically, the idea was that men were oversexed beings. They needed sex and they needed a lot of it, but they weren't particularly discriminating about how they satisfied their sexual needs. If their wives couldn't fulfill their sexual appetites, men would turn to prostitutes and other men; this wasn't considered surprising or unusual during the Victorian era. In this sense, having sex with other men was seen as an expression of masculinity, rather than a contradiction of what it meant to be a man. The idea that men who wanted to have sex with other men might be different or abnormal in some way took time to develop historically.

The gradual evolution of these ideas about what it meant to

be homosexual is what you might call the development of the homosexual role. This is the idea that there are certain expectations beyond just sexual behavior that go along with being homosexual in European-influenced cultures. One of those expectations is that if you're a gay man, you're also feminine. But you're feminine in very specific ways; for example, you're expected to like to gossip like women, but no one expects that you'll be excellent at taking care of babies, which is another feminine trait. The homosexual role as it comes to be defined also assumes that having any attraction to or sexual encounter with another man cancels out any attraction to or sexual encounter with a woman. We would generally consider a man who's been in a sexual and romantic relationship with a woman for many years, but then has a sexual relationship with a man, to be gay. Same-gender desire and behavior effectively erases any heterosexual desire or behavior, but the opposite isn't true. A gay man who has sex with a woman probably won't be considered straight.

In a weird sort of contrast to this rule, the homosexual role also tells us that being gay is a permanent state. You don't switch back and forth between being gay and something else. Even if you don't come out as gay until much later in life, we assume that you were really gay all along. There's very little fluidity in the way homosexuality is constructed in European-influenced cultures.

The connections between sexuality and gender in European-influenced cultures go way back. And as you can see, they're pretty complicated. Regardless of what your sexual identity is, these connections are going to have an effect on you.

- ↗ You are gay. **GO TO 75.**
- ↖ You are straight. **GO TO 79.**
- ↘ You are bisexual. **GO TO 81.**
- ↖ You are asexual. **GO TO 83.**
- → You are demisexual. **GO TO 84.**
- ↘ You are queer. **GO TO 85.**

88

In your culture, sexuality and gender aren't connected. The categories or ways of understanding sexual behavior aren't based on gender. Maybe that sounds weird, but it's not that uncommon. There's no particular reason why gender should be the most important factor in determining who has sex with whom or what kind of sex they have. If you really think about it, gender isn't a particularly good way to organize sexuality. What does knowing someone's gender really tell us about their level of sexual compatibility? For example, say you prefer having sex with someone who has a penis. Gender—in this case, whether or not someone looks and acts in ways that are consistent with masculinity—won't necessarily tell you whether or not that person has a penis. Many quite masculine people don't have a penis. Or maybe you prefer someone who's passive sexually. Should you be attracted to women? That might work out for you, but not all women enjoy being passive in their sexual interactions. You might be really into superhero role-playing as part of your sexual repertoire. Gender isn't going to help you figure out who is or isn't into superheroes.

There are many different ways to potentially organize sexuality that might make a lot more sense than gender. In many cultures, what's most important when categorizing sexuality is power and status. In some contemporary Latin American cultures, certain men who have sex with other men aren't viewed as falling outside the norms for masculine sexual behavior. If two men have sex, the man who is the dominant partner is still considered masculine. This means that a man who is the dominant partner can have sex with women or men and, as long as he maintains his dominance, he won't be viewed as deviant. A man who has sex with another man as the nondominant partner, on the other hand, will be seen as violating the rules for appropriate masculine sexuality. Ultimately, your position of power is more important than the gender of the person you're having sex with.

That's just one alternative way of organizing sexuality around categories other than gender. The possibilities are endless, even if it might be hard to imagine what sex would look like without gender.

↖ To explore a different gender path, **TURN BACK TO 2.**

89

There are a variety of medical avenues that you might pursue as a trans woman, but a lot depends on your age and where you are in relation to puberty. If you're young enough that you haven't hit puberty yet, you might take puberty blockers to prevent the effects of that bodily transformation from taking place. You'll take hormones that prevent your voice from deepening or facial hair from growing.

After puberty, you might start taking hormone treatments that encourage your body to develop in a feminine way. The effects of these hormones are similar to the experience of puberty, so this could be either a first or second puberty for you. As a trans woman, you might take estrogen, testosterone blockers, and progesterones. These hormones will have a wide range of effects on your body.

Physically, your skin might change, becoming drier, thinner, and more sensitive. You may develop breast buds and, eventually, breasts; as with cisgender women, the size and shape of your breasts will vary. You probably won't develop breasts much bigger than an A-cup. The distribution of fat in your body may shift as well, with fat collecting around your hips and thighs. The muscles in your arms and legs will become less developed. The hair on your body will become less thick and grow at a slower rate. It might not go away altogether; remember that even cisgender women sometimes have prominent facial hair.

Your emotional state may or may not change. Changes to the level and type of hormones in your body can cause you to have different sorts of feelings, but emotions are social as well as physiological. Maybe you'll feel more sensitive and more likely to cry. But many cisgender women don't feel this way, so your emotions may be unaffected.

Sexually, you'll have fewer erections as a result of hormone therapy. In addition, your erections won't be as hard or last as long. You will still be able to enjoy sex and have orgasms, though. The orgasms that you do have may feel different, as different parts of your body come to feel erotically sensitive. Your testicles will shrink to almost half their previous size. Finally, your body will probably stop producing sperm, meaning that you're likely to become sterile—incapable of producing children.

You'll be safest if you pursue hormone therapy under the guidance of a doctor or other medical professional, although it is possible to obtain hormones while circumventing the medical route. The drugs used in hormone replacement therapy are available to purchase from online pharmacies and can be obtained without a doctor's prescription. Online discussion pages, such as TransDIY (do-it-yourself) on Reddit, provide information from other transgender people on how to purchase and self-administrate hormone replacement therapy. Some of these online pharmacies are of dubious legality, but as a trans woman, you might pursue this route for two reasons.

First, hormone therapy can be expensive and, depending on where you work, your health insurance might not cover the costs. In 2017, 647 companies in the United States covered healthcare costs for their transgender employees, up from a mere 49 companies in 2009. If you're lucky enough to work for one of those companies, you're more likely to go through a doctor or other medical professional to obtain hormones. But the other reason you might be reluctant to see a doctor is that many are still unsympathetic or outright hostile to transgender patients. This attitude might come from a lack of knowledge about transgender health or from their own cissexism or transphobia.

> **CISSEXISM**
>
> *n.* /ˈsis-ˈsek-ˌsi-zəm/
>
> Prejudice or discrimination against transgender people, or the belief that transgender people are inferior to cisgender people.

Cissexism is prejudice or discrimination against transgender people, while transphobia is a fear or hatred of transgender people. Unfortunately, many doctors and other health professionals are no more immune to cissexism and transphobia than other people are.

In fact, science and medicine as institutions have sometimes contributed to the stigmatization of transgender people. The *Diagnostic and Statistical Manual of Mental Disorders* (*DSM*) is a sort of bible used by psychiatrists and other mental health professionals to diagnose various disorders. First published in 1952, the *DSM* is important because insurance providers use its codes to decide on coverage for various conditions. Basically, the *DSM* codifies certain disorders as real or not. Until 2012,

> **TRANSPHOBIA**
>
> ***n.*** /ˌtranzˈfō-bē-ə/
>
> Hatred for or prejudice against transgender people.

the *DSM* included a category for "gender-identity disorder," described as a mismatch between the gender a person expressed and their assigned gender.

Transgender activists argued that this category made being transgender into a disorder—like the other illnesses in the *DSM* that need to be treated and cured. It made being transgender feel abnormal and stigmatized. In 2012, the DSM removed gender-identity disorder, replacing it with gender dysphoria. Gender dysphoria focuses on the distress caused by the mismatch between a person's gender assignment and gender identity, rather than on the mismatch itself. So the disorder is now defined as the psychological distress caused by societal reaction to being transgender, rather than as being transgender in and of itself.

As a trans woman, you might feel that the changes brought on by hormone therapy create the type of gendered body that fits your sense of who you are. Or you might feel that sex reassignment or gender-confirming surgery is what you need in order to create the right body for yourself. If that's the case, you'll probably have to take hormone treatments for one year before you can have surgery. The process involved in getting access to gender-confirming surgery depends on where you are.

↗ You're in the United States. **GO TO 96.**

↘ You're in Thailand. **GO TO 97.**

90

You decide not to have surgery, because there are as many ways to be a trans woman as there are to be a cisgender woman. A body unaltered by surgery feels okay to you. Maybe you don't take testosterone blockers or estrogen, either. Dressing as a woman, changing your name, and asking people to use feminine pronouns might feel just right to you.

You might find yourself having to explain to other people why you're not having gender-confirming surgery, which is weird. No one tells cisgender people what surgeries they should or shouldn't have, so why do people—both within and outside of the transgender community—feel compelled to tell you what you should or shouldn't do with your body? In fact, the ability to not have people, even sometimes complete strangers, ask you questions about your genitalia, is a good example of a cisgender privilege that you don't have as a trans woman. What you do or don't do with your body should be no one's business but your own, but that's probably not the way it will work.

If you don't have surgery or use hormone therapy, you might find it harder to achieve social femaleness. It might be more difficult for people to interact with you as a woman, because their gender attribution doesn't line up with your feminine gender identity. Gender attribution is the process by which people see you and say, "That's a woman," or "That's a man." We all engage in gender attribution when we see people, drawing on a long list of cues to help us out. What people look like is an important part of gender attribution, but so is who they're with, how they interact, and how much power they have in a given situation. For example, if you see a couple holding hands or kissing, heteronormativity might dictate that you assume one of the people is a man and one of them is a woman. Heteronormativity is the assumption that heterosexuality is normal and right. If you see someone wearing the trappings of power—dressed as a police officer or in the uniform of a high-ranking military officer—you might be more likely to assume that person is a man. These and other cues help us decide on the gender of the people with whom we're interacting.

> **GENDER ATTRIBUTION**
>
> *n.* /ˈjen-dər ˌa-trə-ˈbyü-shən/
>
> The process by which an observer guesses which gender they believe another person to be. Once a person makes an attribution, it can be difficult to change their mind if they happen to be wrong about the person's gender.

We believe that we're pretty good at gender attribution, so most of the time, it's automatic. You don't have to stop and think about the gender of people you see, even if a lot of the time, you might be getting it wrong. Gender attribution usually rises to the surface of our consciousness only when there's some gender ambiguity—when we can't tell for sure what someone's gender is. This is more likely to happen to you, as a trans woman, and not fitting into people's preexisting gender categories can be a dangerous thing. In 2016, twenty-two transgender people were murdered in the United States, and the majority were trans women. Trans women of color are especially vulnerable to violence—almost half of those murders were committed against trans women of color.

As a trans woman, you're at a disadvantage when it comes to gender attribution. Our default mode when we're sorting people into different genders is man. That is, we assume that people are men until something proves us wrong. That means that it might be harder for you to achieve social femaleness— for people to assume that you are a woman and interact with you on the basis of that.

↖ **GO TO 50.**

91

Puberty starts for you before it does for the rest of your friends. Your voice starts to get all squeaky before settling into a deeper range. You get wet dreams at night and embarrassing erections during the day. Hair starts growing in new places (on your face and in your armpits and between your legs). Being first is good.

There are certainly aspects of puberty for boys that can be embarrassing or annoying—like your squeaky voice. But the social meanings attached to this transition are pretty positive for you. To become a man is to become powerful. If you develop earlier than other boys, they'll most likely be jealous of your deeper voice and the way your body starts to bulk up. You might tease the other boys who are lagging behind.

Puberty is one part of how your experience of gender will be embodied, which means that gender as a category interacts with our bodies in important ways. One of those ways is through ability or disability. Gender intersects with the degree to which your body is seen as abled or disabled. In other words, is your body seen as "normal" and capable of doing the things required of bodies in your society, or is it viewed as incapable to some extent of doing the things expected of "normal" bodies?

↗ You have a temporarily abled body. **GO TO 98.**

↘ You have a disabled body. **GO TO 99.**

92

It feels like everyone else's voice is settling into a deeper range, while yours still sounds like a girl's. Your body is still smooth and hairless. Being last sucks.

Boys who hit puberty later are certainly likely to get teased. You and other boys might compare how big your muscles are. If you hit puberty late, you'll probably lose these contests, as you take longer to bulk up in the way boys do around this age. You might start shaving your face even if you haven't started growing any facial hair, because that's what grown men do. Though there are unpleasant aspects of puberty for boys, becoming a man is generally seen as a good thing. It's something you'll probably look forward to eagerly, even if it comes a little later.

Puberty is one part of how your experience of gender will be embodied, which means that gender as a category interacts with our bodies in important ways. One of those ways is through ability or disability. Gender intersects with the degree to which your body is seen as abled or disabled. In other words, is your body seen as "normal" and capable of doing the things required of bodies in your society, or is it viewed as incapable to some extent of doing the things expected of "normal" bodies?

↗ You have a temporarily abled body. **GO TO 98.**

↘ You have a disabled body. **GO TO 99.**

93

You have a temporarily abled body. Your body is only temporarily able because at some point in our lives, all of us will be differently abled. You'll break a bone and need to use crutches. You'll hurt your back and walk slower than you used to. If you grow old enough, your mobility will eventually become limited. As a woman, if you become pregnant, certain restrictions will be put on you, and your body will, for several months, be unable to do many of the things that it usually can.

Pointing to the temporary nature of ability helps to highlight the way in which disability itself is socially constructed. That means that we create the boundaries and norms that make up what it means to be differently abled. Many people are unable to use steps. But if we lived in a culture where we made all of our buildings without steps, using elevators or ramps instead, many of these people would suddenly not be defined as differently abled or disabled. Some people are seen as disabled or differently abled because they can't process written information as well as they can oral information. In a world where information was equally available in both formats, they would no longer be classified this way. The way we structure our society draws the lines between who is and isn't seen as differently abled or disabled.

Nevertheless, for now you have a body that is defined as able. That doesn't mean that your experience of gender isn't still deeply tied to the type of body you have and what your culture tells you about that body.

> ↗ You feel good about your body. **GO TO 111.**
>
> ↘ You feel bad about your body. **GO TO 112.**

94

You have a disabled body, and that can mean a lot of different things. You might have a physical disability, which means that your body is incapable of accomplishing some tasks defined as essential in your particular society. Maybe you're paralyzed and can't walk. Maybe you have bad knees and can't use stairs. Maybe you're blind or deaf. You might also have a learning disability. Maybe you're dyslexic and have trouble reading. Perhaps you have a mental disability, or you're developmentally delayed.

Regardless of the particular disability you have, your experience of that disability will be shaped by the fact that you're a woman. As a disabled woman, you'll find it harder to live up to the beauty ideal for women in places like the United States. The beauty ideal is an ever-changing but always unobtainable standard for what women should look like in order to be seen as attractive and, in many ways, worthy. The important thing to remember about the beauty ideal is that everyone falls short. If your disability is visible, you're even more likely to fall short of those standards. Disabled people in general are perceived as people who are neither sexually desirable nor particularly interested in sex themselves.

It will be difficult for you to keep these messages about the desirability of your body from affecting the way you feel about yourself. But your experiences of gender will remain deeply tied to your bodily experiences.

↗ You feel good about your body. **GO TO 111.**

↘ You feel bad about your body. **GO TO 112.**

95

You like gender the way it is and think it should stay the same. You might argue, *Hey, it's a lot better than it used to be, right?* In some ways, yes. In other ways, no.

We like to believe that history is a straight line moving upward in terms of progress—including our views about gender. We want to believe that things just keep getting better, but that isn't necessarily the case. The gender pay gap, or the difference between the average income of women and men, has pretty much stalled in the last thirty years. Even though more women than men are graduating from high school, college, and graduate school, so far those gains aren't translating into women making more money. Some people argue that with the spread of European-influenced ideas about gender to the rest of the world, gender inequality has actually gotten worse, rather than better, over time. And people who don't fit into society's neat categories of cisgender, heterosexual male or female struggle every day with a lack of understanding and acceptance, as well as unequal access to opportunities and even some of the basic civil rights that many people take for granted.

Maybe gender as a social system now is better than it was in the past, but it's fairly certain that things won't stay the same. History doesn't work that way, and there's always the chance that things will get worse instead of better.

↗ Pick another gender ending: **TURN TO 148.**

↘ Or **GO TO THE END** to read the conclusion.

96

In the United States, gaining access to gender-confirming surgery is a long and complicated process. You'll first have to be diagnosed with gender dysphoria, which means that you'll have to convince a psychiatrist or other mental health professional that the mismatch between your gender assignment and gender identity are causing you serious distress. This also means that the decision about whether gender-confirming surgery is right for you isn't yours alone.

In the 1960s through about the 1980s, the process by which doctors decided who was allowed to have sex-reassignment surgery and who wasn't could be somewhat arbitrary. As a trans woman, your surgery was more likely to be approved if you already looked like a feminine man. One physician at Johns Hopkins, one of the handful of hospitals that performed sex-reassignment surgery in the mid to late twentieth century, described bullying trans women who came to him seeking surgery. He would use their reactions to decide whether they were truly in need of the procedure: he claimed that true trans women would cry, while gay men would get aggressive. Physicians like him served as gatekeepers, but as word spread through transgender communities, those seeking surgery learned what they should and shouldn't say in order to be approved.

In the United States today, you'll probably have to live as a woman for a period of time before your surgery. If your doctor follows the World Professional Association for Transgender Health (WPATH) standards of care, you'll have to live as a woman for a whole year before having gender-confirming surgery, though some experts and patients consider those standards too strict. During this year, you'll change your name and go through all aspects of your daily life living as a woman. At the end of it, you'll have to prove to your surgeon that you have been successfully living as a woman.

What does it mean to "live successfully" as a woman? In the past, WPATH standards of care used a list of set criteria to judge your success living as another gender. You had to undertake some combination of maintaining full-time or part-time employment, functioning as a student, or volunteering in a community-based activity. In other words, you couldn't hide in your house for a year and successfully live as a woman. You were also required to acquire a legal, gender-appropriate name and to provide documentation that someone besides your therapist knew that you were functioning in your new gender. So you'd have to adopt a "feminine" name and get someone to testify to the fact that you've been living as a woman. These criteria might seem a bit excessive, and in 2011, the standards of care were revised to be more ambiguous. They now require "twelve continuous months of living in a gender role that is congruent with their gender identity." What that means is left up to individual therapists and surgeons to decide.

Once you've cleared all those hurdles, you'll be able to have gender-confirming surgery. Your surgery will most likely involve the removal of your testicles and most of your penis. Your urethra will also be shortened (cisgender women have shorter urethras then cisgender men), and some of the skin from your testicles will be used to create a functioning vagina. A clitoris of sorts can also be created from your penis that retains some sexual sensation. You'll keep your prostate. The alterations to your genitalia make up what's sometimes called bottom surgery. You might also elect to get top surgery, which means breast implants. Some trans women also have surgery to remove or reduce their Adam's apple or to change their facial structure to look more feminine. You might also have certain types of surgical procedures while forgoing others. Maybe you decide on bottom surgery but elect against breast implants. Or vice versa.

↖ **GO TO 50.**

97

You're not alone in heading to Thailand for your gender-confirming surgery—it's one of the world's most popular destinations for transgender people seeking this medical procedure. At just one of the nearly two dozen gender clinics in Thailand, surgeons perform two to three gender operations per week. As of 2015, there were at least one hundred Thai doctors qualified to perform gender-confirming surgery.

Why is Thailand such a popular destination for gender-confirming surgery? The surgery is much cheaper in Thailand than it is in many other places; it costs about a third of what it would in the United States. And there are a lot more clinics and doctors available in Thailand to perform your surgery.

You'll also find it a much quicker process to get gender-confirming surgery in Thailand than in the United States and many other countries. It takes less time in Thailand because, unlike in the United States, there's no protocol requiring you to live for a year as a woman before you can have access to gender-confirming surgery. Doctors in the United States and other places that follow the WPATH (World Professional

Association for Transgender Health) standards of care would require you to demonstrate your full commitment before surgery by living as a woman, but this isn't the case in Thailand.

Your gender-confirming surgery will most likely involve the removal of your testicles and most of your penis. Your urethra will also be shortened (cisgender women have shorter urethras then cisgender men), and some of the skin from your testicles will be used to create a functioning vagina. A clitoris of sorts can also be created from your penis that retains some sexual sensation. You'll keep your prostate. The alterations to your genitalia make up what's sometimes called bottom surgery. You might also elect to get top surgery, which means breast implants. Some trans women also have surgery to remove or reduce their Adam's apple or to change their facial structure to look more feminine. You might also have certain types of surgical procedures while forgoing others. Maybe you decide on bottom surgery but elect against breast implants. Or vice versa.

↖ **GO TO 50.**

↑ ↗

98

You're a temporarily able-bodied man. Your body is only temporarily able because at some point in our lives, all of us will be differently abled. You'll break a bone and go on crutches. You'll hurt your back and walk slower than you used to. If you grow old enough, your mobility will eventually become limited. As a man, those periods when your body isn't fully functional in all the ways it's supposed to be might be especially difficult. After all, able-bodied is really what all men are supposed to be. In fact, you might argue that calling yourself a man already implies that you have a strong and capable body. Without such a body, you might not feel like a man at all. Masculinity, from this perspective, seems deeply tied to bodies.

There's some question, when it comes to the issue of bodies, as to whether women or men are more connected to their bodies. Traditionally, if you line up the dualities of mind and body with masculine and feminine, women would be viewed as belonging to the body side of that divide. Men are supposed to have all the qualities associated with the mind—they're rational, logical, and objective. Women get all the messier bodily stuff. Women are seen as more emotional and enslaved to their bodies through menstruation, pregnancy, and childbirth.

These associations between men and the mind and women and the body aren't neutral; they potentially benefit you as a man. Usually, someone who is logical and rational is seen as superior to someone who is ruled by their emotions. This is the argument often used to prevent women from occupying positions of power and leadership—like being president. They're too emotional and ruled by their bodies—their periods or menopause or hormones in whatever form.

That you line up on the mind side of this duality could benefit you as a man, but it doesn't mean that your body is completely unimportant. As a man, you need to have the right kind of body—one that's capable of doing the things a man's body should do. You're lucky to have one of those, at least for now. But how do you feel about that able body you're lucky enough to find yourself in?

↗ You feel good about your body. **GO TO 116.**

↘ You feel bad about your body. **GO TO 117.**

99

Your experience of masculinity will be shaped in a wide range of ways by your disability. If you've had your disability since birth, it may have shaped the type of gender socialization that you received. Your parents and others may not have expected the same things of you as a boy that they would have expected from a son without a disability. For example, if you have a physical disability that prevents you from playing sports, that part of your socialization as a boy may have been different.

In addition, if you have a disability that affects how well you learn and understand, it might be harder for people to hold you accountable to gender expectations. Gender is a fairly complicated concept for children to master, even without some sort of disability. If you suffer from a severe intellectual disability, punishing and rewarding you for masculine behaviors won't have the same effect as it would on someone without your condition.

An important role laid out for you as a man is to have a job and be a breadwinner—someone who supports a family though his income. Your disability will make it more difficult to fulfill this aspect of masculinity. Depending on your disability, you may be unable to work. If you do work, you're likely to be paid much less as a differently abled or disabled man, though you'll still do better than women in this group.

Your disability may intersect with what it means for you to be a man in a variety of ways. But there's more to your relationship with your body than just whether you're able-bodied or not.

↗ You feel good about your body. **GO TO 116.**

↘ You feel bad about your body. **GO TO 117.**

100

You believe that gender is okay, but what we need to change is gender inequality. This is what many feminists believe, so feel free to call yourself one.

Can you separate the idea of gender from the idea of inequality? That's a big question that feminists and other people who study gender argue about. One side of the argument claims that we can have differences without necessarily having a sense of inequality. The two don't have to go hand in hand. Men and women don't have to be the same in order for there to be equality. In fact, some people might argue that it's impossible for women and men to be the same, anyway. From this perspective, gender difference does not automatically lead to gender inequality. So we can keep gender while making the world more equal.

But others argue that as soon as we begin to talk about differences, inequality inevitably follows. When we divide the world into dichotomies, one side is always assumed to be better than the other—black and white aren't just two different colors. White is also seen as better than black. This is true of all the big dichotomies in our thinking: body/mind, emotional/ rational, woman/man, transgender/cisgender, and so on. That's sort of the point of difference in the first place. You can't just say that men are more rational and women are more emotional without also assuming that one of those is better than the other. Difference always leads to inequality.

Gender is a category that we made up, and it's about much more than our anatomy or how we dress or who we desire. The fact is that part of the point of gender as a category is to create inequality. Gender was constructed in order to distribute power in an uneven way. So if we want to truly get rid of inequality, gender itself will have to go.

↗ Pick a different gender ending: **GO TO 148.**

↘ Or **GO TO THE END** to check out the conclusion.

101

You're in luck. Because of heteronormativity, most systems of courtship and dating that have existed over time and across cultures were designed with you in mind. It might not seem easy to you, but in most places, the process of finding someone to love or marry is almost totally geared toward people like you.

↗ You live in a culture where calling is the dominant system of courtship. **GO TO 122.**

↖ You live in a culture where dating is the dominant system of courtship. **GO TO 123.**

↘ You live in a culture where hookups are the dominant system of courtship. **GO TO 124.**

↙ →

102

You don't want to pursue a sexual relationship, but that doesn't necessarily mean that you don't want to hold hands or cuddle on the couch and watch Netflix with someone. As many asexual individuals point out, those two things—wanting to have sex and wanting to have a deep, intimate attachment to another person—don't have to go together. If you're asexual and romantic, you might still describe yourself as straight, gay, lesbian, or bisexual, depending on the gender of the people you find romantically attractive. You might be quite happy in a relationship with someone else who's okay with not having sex. Or you might engage in some sexual behavior for the benefit of the person with whom you're in a relationship.

How do you go about finding someone to be in a relationship with as an asexual, romantic person?

↖ **GO TO 65.**

103

You don't want to have a sexual or a romantic relationship with anyone. Wanting to have sex and wanting to have a deep, intimate attachment to another person don't necessarily have to go together. But you don't want either. That doesn't mean that you might not still think of yourself as bisexual, lesbian, or gay. In fact, many asexual, aromantic people do identify themselves in these ways. They may be in companionate relationships with people of the same gender or a different gender or both. That means that they may spend time with someone and enjoy their company, but they're not necessarily in love with and don't want to have sex with that person.

How do you go about finding someone to be in a relationship with as an asexual, aromantic person?

↖ **GO TO 65.**

104

You might assume that you're in one of the twenty-five countries (as of this writing) in which same-gender marriage is currently legal. In these countries, you'll have access to most of the legal protections that come with marriage. You won't have to worry about whether your spouse will be allowed into your hospital room when you're sick or injured. If you have health insurance through your employer, your spouse will be covered too. You can be assured that if one of you dies, the other will inherit. You can, as a married couple, more easily adopt children. You will benefit from all the perks that come from marriage as a social institution.

You might be living in one of those countries in the present day, but you might also be in any one of several historic societies where same-gender marriage was also accepted. Same-gender marriage isn't a totally new, twenty-first-century thing. Elderly women in some African cultures were allowed to take younger women for their wives; these marriages were not sexual, but legal and social arrangements. They allowed elderly women to have the power and comfort that comes with having a wife. Between 1865 and 1935, women in China's Pearl River Delta formed intimate sisterhoods among silk workers. Their economic independence allowed them to resist traditional marriage and instead form relationships with other women. Within the sisterhood, the women viewed these relationships as marriages, carrying with them the same family structure and rules of a traditional heterosexual marriage. During the Ming dynasty in China, women would become bound to younger women in elaborate wedding ceremonies. These are just a few examples of historical time periods in which some form of same-gender marriage existed.

Contemporary same-gender marriages have the potential to make marriage a much less gendered space. In general, it seems that same-gender marriages are more egalitarian than heterosexual marriages in terms of sharing housework and childcare responsibilities.

Regardless of the particular type of marriage you're in or how you decide who takes out the trash, you'll find that race and ethnicity will overlap with your gender in important ways.

↖ **GO TO 78.**

105

There are lots of reasons why you might never get married. How your permanently single status is viewed will depend on the culture you find yourself in.

- ↗ You're an unmarried person in China. **GO TO 118.**
- ↖ You're an unmarried person in Denmark. **GO TO 119.**
- ↘ You're an unmarried person in the United States. **GO TO 120.**

106

The stigma against being an unmarried woman in the United States is much higher than that attached to being an unmarried man. That this is true is evident in the language asymmetry that exists around men and women's marital status. A language asymmetry is when some aspect of language reflects and helps to shape an inequality. The titles given to married women and married men are one example of a language asymmetry. Both married and single men are referred to as "Mr." in American English. But women's titles are distinguished on the basis of their marital status, so that a married woman is "Mrs." while an unmarried woman is "Miss." The title "Ms." was suggested as an alternative as early as 1901 and then championed by feminists in the 1970s. "Ms." is meant to be used as the equivalent of "Mr."—as a generic title that doesn't denote a woman's marital status—but the use of "Ms." has never become widespread.

> **LANGUAGE ASYMMETRY**
>
> *n.* /ˈlaŋ-gwij, -wij (ˌ)ā-ˈsi-mə-trē/
>
> An aspect of language that reflects and shapes an inequality.

Language asymmetries reveal important aspects of inequality. In this example, you can see how it's culturally more important to identify a woman's marital status than it is to know whether a man is married. In other words, women are defined partly by their relationship to men, while men are not defined in terms of their relationship to women.

Which brings us to the language asymmetry connected to single women. We have words that are specific to an unmarried woman—spinster and old maid. Neither of those words have positive connotations. What do we call an unmarried man? A bachelor, a word that has none of the negative associations of spinster and old maid. In fact, to be a bachelor is usually seen as a good thing. In other words, bachelor and spinster aren't equivalent words. They tell us very different things about what it means to be an unmarried man compared to what it means to be an unmarried woman. The only way we can get close to a positive word for an unmarried woman is to create a feminine version of bachelor—bachelorette.

↖ **GO TO 78.**

107

In the United States, there's much less stigma attached to not being married for you as a guy than there would be if you were a woman. In fact, it might be seen as kind of cool. Think of the fictional character who served as a spokesman for Dos Equis beer: The Most Interesting Man in the World. The man was clearly older and theoretically a bachelor. Those characteristics made him dangerous, sexy, and interesting. It's hard to imagine a feminine equivalent—a woman in her late fifties or early sixties who's never been married but is still seen as sexy and glamorous.

The different ways in which being single as a man and being single as a woman are viewed tells us a lot about how masculinity and femininity are defined. Men are supposed to want to be independent and free from the bonds of marriage. To some extent, being single as a man is your natural state. Women, on the other hand, are unlikely to choose to stay single voluntarily. If a woman reaches a certain age and hasn't been married, she's a spinster, a word that implies that she's single not because she wants to be, but because she failed some essential test of femininity.

↖ **GO TO 78.**

↙ →

108

You think gender is basically a stupid idea. Or maybe just that it's harmful. Or that it comes with too many rules. Something about gender makes you believe that it needs to go. What would a world without gender look like?

At first, people assume that in a world without gender, everyone would be the same. That doesn't have to be the case, though. Gender as a system actually forces us to suppress some of our uniqueness in order to fit into a category. So you could argue that without gender, people would be more different. Here's how the radical feminist and writer, John Stoltenberg, imagines what a world without gender might look like in his essay, "How Men Have (a) Sex."

When a baby's born, no one would ask whether it's a boy or a girl. Everyone in this world knows that such things don't exist. There are people with XX chromosomes and people with XY chromosomes and people with XO and XXY and XYY chromosomes. There are a lot of possibilities for what your chromosomes could look like and, in this world, that's seen as a good thing. When a baby is born with some fairly rare combination of chromosomes, everyone celebrates the infant's individuality as sign of how unique they all are.

In this world, everyone knows that there is a wide range of genital formations too. They also understand that all those structures and organs exist along a continuum. It's a complicated gradation from people with a vulva and a clitoris to those with a penis and a scrotal sac. In other words, people's genitals show that there are many more than just two types of people. There are, in fact, infinite types of people. Those differences are just another sign of everyone's uniqueness. What's more, these organs all started out as the same thing—genital tubercles. So in this world, people understand that one person's genital tubercle might be different from another person's genital tubercle, but all genital tubercles are capable of giving people some sort of sexual pleasure. All that individuality doesn't divide people so much as make them feel connected.

In this world, there are no sex hormones. The chemical substances that we, under our current gender system, call sex hormones are instead known as "individuality inducers." Individuality inducers do the exact same things as sex hormones, but the way in which they're understood is different. In this world, individuality inducers make everyone uniquely different—they don't create people who have to fit into one of two groups. Some people in this world can become pregnant and some people can't, but fertility isn't determined solely by chromosomes or genitals or hormones. It would be silly to make too big of a deal out of any of these things that make people unique. Why base a whole category around something so silly as what people have between their legs? In this world, the amazing variety that nature gives everyone is celebrated.

As Stoltenberg points out, everything about the physical reality of this imagined world is true in our own world. There are infinite variations in how biological gender is expressed at the chromosomal, anatomical, and hormonal level. But we make sense of that variation differently. We try to cram all of that diversity into just two categories, instead of celebrating how truly unique we all are.

In this particular, imagined world without gender, we'd all be free to express our individuality without having to force ourselves into categories of masculinity or femininity. There would be no women or men, just completely and totally unique individuals.

↗ Pick a different gender ending: **GO TO 148.**

↘ Or **GO TO THE END** to check out the conclusion.

109

Lucky you! You get to choose the person you marry. You get to fall in love and find the person who's your soul mate. The person who's your best friend. In a companionate marriage, the expectation is just that—your spouse is also your companion. Maybe this seems normal to you, but in the grand sweep of human history, companionate marriage is pretty weird. Also, you might argue that it doesn't work very well. Divorce rates in countries with companionate marriages are much higher than those with different types of marriage.

On the other hand, if you're a woman, you have more freedom in a companionate marriage. This is especially true in the contemporary United States. Up until the 1970s, so-called head and master laws still gave men much more power in a marriage. Before these laws were abolished, as a man, you could move your family without your wife's consent. There was no such thing as marital rape, since the laws assumed that marriage implied consent. There was also no such thing as domestic violence, as a man had the right to treat his wife and children however he wanted. Being able to marry the person you fall in love with might seem like a good thing, but it doesn't guarantee that everything will work out.

Even today, companionate marriages can be deeply gendered from the get-go. Take weddings, for example. Although many couples now write their own vows, some still speak traditional versions where brides promise to "honor and obey" their husbands. Most traditional wedding ceremonies are both gendered and heteronormative. There's a bride and a groom, along with bridesmaids and groomsmen. The father, not the mother, is the one who "gives" the bride away. Many women take their husband's name when they get married.

You don't have to follow all the gender rules laid out for marriage, but because they're still seen as normal, you might be questioned for breaking them.

↖ **GO TO 78.**

110

In a culture with traditional marriage, you will most likely get married, but love probably won't have much to do with it. Getting married to someone you love is seen as foolish and maybe even dangerous. Marriage is about forming alliances or gaining wealth. So your marriage will probably be set up for you, usually by your family. You might meet your spouse beforehand. It's more likely that you won't.

This is the way that marriage worked for long periods of human history. With some variations, it's still how marriage works in some places. In arranged marriages, the expectation might be that you'll fall in love with your spouse after you're married. But falling in love isn't necessary to a successful marriage.

If you're a woman living in a culture like this, you'll probably have little power to decide who you marry and very little power once you are married. You're part of the property being exchanged in an economic interaction—a daughter in exchange for a peace treaty or a piece of land. In many of these cultures, women are the goods being exchanged and men are the ones doing the deal-making. The children you might have will be seen as belonging to their father and under his control.

↖ **GO TO 78.**

111

You have positive feelings about your body, which is a good thing and also a fairly rare thing among women and girls. Maybe you feel good about your body because you participate in sports. Girls and women who play sports report having more positive feelings about their bodies in general. Sports seem to help with body image, because through sports, girls and women are able to see their bodies as an active subject, rather than as a passive object. That means that if you play sports, your body acts on other things—your body hits a ball or runs fast or dives smoothly. Your body has uses that are about much more than just how it looks to other people.

When your body is an object, it becomes something that's acted upon. People look at your body or talk about your body. They decide whether your body is desirable or not. They touch your body. When your body is an object, its worth comes from external sources. You may lose weight or wear more makeup or have cosmetic surgery to change your body, but in the end, if your body is an object, other people are the ones who decide whether it's satisfactory or not. So maybe part of why you feel good about your body is that you're able to see it as more than an object.

How you feel about your body will also come into play as you explore your sexuality. The first question to ask about your sexuality is not how you identify sexually, but how sexuality is structured in the society you live in.

- ↗ You live in a culture where gender and sexuality are connected. **GO TO 50.**
- ↘ You live in a culture where gender and sexuality are not connected. **GO TO 131.**

112

You don't feel so great about your body. Welcome to the club. Most women and girls don't have positive feelings about their bodies. Many girls begin to lose their sense of satisfaction with their bodies at puberty. There are lots of reasons why this happens. Puberty is when many girls whose gender expression may have been less than perfect—girls who were tomboys—are pressured to start conforming more closely to gender expectations. Puberty is also when many girls are cautioned about the world of sexuality and all the dangers that it holds for them. The fear of being assaulted is real, and so is the careful line that women must negotiate between being sexually active and being labeled too promiscuous.

It's also at puberty that what some feminists call "the third shift" begins to kick in for girls. If the first shift is paid work outside the home and the second shift is the extra housework and childcare duties that women are expected to do, then the third shift is the beauty work that women are increasingly obligated to do. This third shift, some feminists argue, serves as a tool to subvert women's increasing power. As women have made significant gains in many areas of social life, the expectations for them be beautiful have increased proportionally. The third shift is part of a backlash intended to derail women's success by diverting their time, energy, and money away from career advancement and by lowering their self-confidence at the same time. The third shift dictates that girls spend a great deal of time and effort altering their bodies (by applying the right sort of makeup, shaving in the right places, painting their nails, using the correct hair-styling products, and losing weight). As with any ideal, the new beauty standards set for girls are unattainable.

That girls see their bodies as a full-time job in need of constant alteration and enhancement might not seem like such a big deal. But the poor body image that results from comparing yourself to the beauty ideal is associated with low self-esteem. And many women risk their health and well-being in the constant quest to measure up to this impossible yardstick. Women develop eating disorders like anorexia and bulimia or engage in other harmful dieting behaviors. By pursuing cosmetic surgery or using a range of beauty products that are largely unregulated and unmonitored for their long-term health effects, they risk exposing themselves to a host of dangers. As far as the economic costs go, as a woman, you'll spend an average of $300,000 on your makeup and other facial beauty products—and that's just for your face—over the course of your life.

How you feel about your body will also come into play as you explore your sexuality. The first question to ask about your sexuality is not how you identify sexually, but how sexuality is structured in the society you live in.

- ↗ You live in a culture where gender and sexuality are connected. **GO TO 50.**
- ↘ You live in a culture where gender and sexuality are not connected. **GO TO 131.**

113

You're going to do some kind of work in your life, regardless of your gender. Your gender will determine the kind of work you do, how the work you do is viewed, and whether or not you get paid for it. Your racial and ethnic background, along with your social class, will also shape your experience of work in important ways.

↗ You're a woman of color or a white working-class woman. **GO TO 125.**

↖ You're a white middle-class or upper-class woman. **GO TO 126.**

↘ You're a woman who doesn't work for pay outside the home. **GO TO 127.**

↖ You're a man who doesn't work for pay outside the home. **GO TO 128.**

→ You're a man who works for pay outside the home. **GO TO 129.**

↖ You're a trans man who works for pay outside the home. **GO TO 130.**

↘ You're a trans woman who works for pay outside the home. **GO TO 142.**

114

There's a long history in the United States of poor women of all racial groups falling victim to forced sterilization, and it's a history that for many women is entirely too recent. Sterilization laws used to be common in the United States—existing in 32 states—and were motivated by crude theories of human inheritance. The laws purportedly attempted to eliminate criminality, feeble-mindedness, and sexual deviance from the population. As the groups most vulnerable to these medical interventions, poor women and women of color were frequent victims of sterilization programs.

California led the country in the number of forced sterilizations that took place between 1909 and 1932. During that period, twenty thousand women and men were sterilized in state institutions, often without their consent or knowledge. In the 1960s and '70s, Mexican American women were sterilized under duress at the Los Angeles County–USC Medical Center. As many as 20 to 25 percent of Native American women in the United States were sterilized between 1970 and 1976, and some of those programs continued into the 1980s. As recently as 2010, California prisons authorized the sterilization of 150 female inmates.

↖ **GO TO 148.**

115

Your access to birth control will vary a great deal depending on where you are.

↗ You're in the United States. **GO TO 154.**

↘ You're outside the United States. **GO TO 155.**

116

You feel good about your body as a boy or a man. That probably means that you conform to the ideals held up for what the perfect man in your particular society or culture should be, many of which have to do with what your body should look like. Here's a list that sociologist Erving Goffman came up with in 1963 to describe the "perfect" man in the United States. He should be young, married, white, urban, northern, heterosexual, Protestant, a father, college-educated, and fully employed, and he should have a good complexion, be of the right weight (not fat), be of the right height (tall), and have recently played sports. Maybe you're lucky enough to have a body that is young, white, acne- and scar-free, fit, tall, and athletic, which is why you feel great about your body.

As a man, you might still feel good about your body even if you can't check off all the criteria on the list above. You can feel good about your body even if you don't feel like it's perfect. You're more likely than women and girls to feel good about your body. That's partly because men are encouraged to think of their bodies as active—as subjects instead of objects.

You've seen these messages about your active body in advertisements and other media depictions since you were a little boy. When girls and women are depicted in advertising, they're often depicted as passive objects. Only one part of their body—often their breasts or their butt—is shown. In many ads, parts of women's bodies are transformed into objects—women's legs become a pair of scissors. When whole women are depicted instead of just parts of their bodies, they're generally doing passive things—lying on a bed or sitting around. These ads convey the ideas that what matters about women are their bodies, and their bodies are objects—things to which something is done.

Ads that feature men like you depict masculine bodies doing things. They depict men as subjects instead of objects. Men play a sport or give a presentation in a conference room. They stand with their legs spread wide staring defiantly at the camera. Though this has changed somewhat in advertising, men are still much more likely to be pictured as active subjects.

When you think of your body as active, it's easier to feel good about it. Your body is good because it can do useful things like hit a ball or run fast or jump high. You don't have to depend on external standards to judge how you feel about your body as much as women do. Sure, you might still worry about how you look in that pair of pants and whether people think you're too short. Men still have standards against which their bodies are judged. But because you're encouraged to think of your body as more than just an object, it's a little easier to feel good about it.

How you feel about your body will also come into play as you explore your sexuality. The first question to ask about your sexuality is not how you identify sexually, but how sexuality is structured in the society you live in.

- ↗ You live in a culture where gender and sexuality are connected. **GO TO 87.**
- ↘ You live in a culture where gender and sexuality are not connected. **GO TO 88.**

117

You feel bad about your body. That might be because you don't live up to the characteristics for the ideal masculine body in your particular time and place. Maybe you feel like you're too skinny. Or you can't grow a beard. Or you're too short.

In places like the United States, it's not surprising that you don't feel good about your body if you're a short man. Being tall is pretty important for men. Studies show that people tend to equate height in men with things like intelligence and competency. That is, people think you're smarter and all around better at stuff if you're taller. And, of course, height is also associated with attractiveness for men.

The weird thing is that the beliefs people have about tall men can actually become true. So if you're taller, you actually are likely to be smarter and more competent. That's not because the traits for intelligence and height are genetically linked. It's because if you believe what other people believe about you, then it becomes a self-fulfilling prophecy—a belief or prediction that comes true solely because it's been predicted. Because people believe that tall men are smarter and more competent, they treat them as if they are smarter and more competent. As a tall man, you see those qualities reflected back at you all the time, like a really amazing mirror being held up to you. And if everyone is always telling you how smart and competent you are, you begin to believe it. You act as if you are smart and competent, which is half the battle of actually becoming smart and competent.

If you're not tall though, you probably won't feel as great about your body, and your self-confidence in general might be lower. You'll move through the world differently as a man with a body that doesn't conform to masculine ideals.

How you feel about your body will also come into play as you explore your sexuality. The first question to ask about your sexuality is not how you identify sexually, but how sexuality is structured in the society you live in.

↗ You live in a culture where gender and sexuality are con-nected. **GO TO 87.**

↘ You live in a culture where gender and sexuality are not connected. **GO TO 88.**

118

In some cultures, the penalties for being unmarried are fairly high. That's usually because marriage is seen as necessary to completing some important steps in your life cycle. For example, in China it's important to have children so that they can take care of you in your old age. Taking care of your parents traditionally was an obligation that was much more institutionalized in Chinese culture than it was in places like the United States. In China, the stigma against leaving your parents to fend for themselves as they grew older was much higher.

But there's also a very large stigma in Chinese society against having children out of wedlock. So if you want to have children to take care of you in your old age, you need to get married first. That makes marriage almost compulsory for people in Chinese society—it's something they have to do.

If you're unmarried in contemporary China, you're very likely to be a man. That's because there's a huge marriage squeeze for men in China. A marriage squeeze happens when some sort of population shift reduces the number of available marriage partners. The marriage squeeze in China means that there are many more men of marrying age than there are women available to marry them. This imbalance is the combined result of the country's former one-child policy and the cultural preference for sons. The one-child policy, a government program that was in place from 1980 through 2015, limited many Chinese families to having only one child. Under this policy, many parents elected to abort female fetuses so they could have sons instead. Newborn daughters were often abandoned or placed for foreign adoption. Over time, these patterns of behavior resulted in a population with 33.59 million more women than men in 2016. In China, 48.55 percent of the population is female compared to a global average of 49.55. By 2020, thirty million men will reach adulthood in China without any women available to marry them.

Those who study changes in population both inside and outside China are concerned about the effects of this marriage squeeze on Chinese society as a whole. Millions of young men with no marriage prospects can be a dangerous situation. Experts predict effects on crime rates, drug use, and violence as these young men face life with no prospect of marriage.

↖ **GO TO 78.**

119

If you're not married in a place like Denmark, it's probably no big deal. That's especially true if, instead of being married, you're in a cohabiting relationship. It's fairly common in Denmark for couples to live together and have children without ever getting married. Among those over the age of twenty, 14 percent lived in a consensual union in Denmark in 2011. This is higher than the average for the entire European Union, at 8.8 percent of the population. Some of these couples may get married eventually, but it's not a big deal if they don't. Many of the laws in Denmark and other Scandinavian countries have changed to reflect this emerging reality, granting cohabiting spouses some of the same considerations usually given to married couples.

If you live in a place like Denmark where fewer people are getting married, it might be a sign of a larger transition in marriage as an institution. Perhaps people don't see marriage as particularly important or necessary anymore.

↖ **GO TO 78.**

120

In the United States, most people eventually get married, even with the high rates of divorce. Even people who divorce mostly end up marrying again. Still, if you never get married, you probably won't be viewed as a complete freak. When you're younger, it won't be seen as that unusual that you're not married. The average age at first marriage in the United States has been creeping steadily upward for years now. Currently, the average age is twenty-seven for women and twenty-nine for men. That's up from twenty and twenty-two, respectively, in 1960.

If you make it into your fifties and sixties without ever having been married, people might start to wonder why. This might be true even if you're in a committed relationship with someone and living with that person. In places like the United States, it's less accepted to settle into a long-term relationship without also getting married. Exactly how weird it is for you to not be married will vary depending on your gender.

↗ You're a woman. **GO TO 106.**

↘ You're a man. **GO TO 107.**

↙ →

121

You occupy multiple identities at the same time. You don't stop being a woman or a lesbian or Arab American at any particular moment. This is part of what people mean when they talk about intersectionality. Everyone experiences their lives at the intersection of many different identities. Gender isn't the only identity that matters.

In your case, your gender and your sexual identity might complicate your Arab American background. This will more likely be true if you're a first- or second-generation immigrant. That is, if you moved to the United States from another country with your parents (first generation) or if your parents moved here and you were born in the United States (second generation). Your family might associate your homosexuality with the influence of white, American culture. As Nadine Naber describes, based on her research on Arab American femininities, your parents might argue that you never would have been a lesbian in the country from which you immigrated. They might say that there is no such thing as homosexuality in their home country. In fact, like many people in non-Western parts of the world, they may claim that homosexuality itself is an American or Western phenomenon. For you, being a lesbian might be perceived by your family as a betrayal of your ethnic and national identity, in a way that might not be true for women of other backgrounds.

Your experience reveals a facet of gender and sexual identity that might remain invisible to those from other racial and ethnic backgrounds—gender and sexual identity are racialized. These identities interact with race and ethnicity, regardless of whether you're Arab American, African American, Native American, Latinx, or white. Gender and sexual identities can also be used to draw racial and ethnic boundaries: the idea that we, as a certain racial or ethnic group, are different from another racial or ethnic group because of how we do gender or sexuality.

↖ **GO TO 65.**

122

If you live in the early nineteenth century in places like the United States, you'll never go on a date, regardless of whether you're a woman or a man. Instead, you'll either call on someone or be called on. During this time period, men court women by obtaining permission from the mother of the woman they are interested in to visit or call. If you don't get permission from the young woman's mother, you aren't allowed to call. Your courtship is dead in the water before it even has a chance to begin. If you're lucky enough to get permission, you and your young lady can sit in the parlor or on the porch, under the supervision of another adult—your chaperone. You aren't allowed to bring gifts. In fact, to do so would be seen as rude and presumptuous—a definite violation of the rules of calling. That's because bringing a woman a gift before you're married to her presumes that she is obligated to you in some way. She owes you, and a gift implies some sense that the debt will be returned sexually. A woman's reputation could be ruined by accepting gifts or money from a suitor.

So, you don't need money to call on a young woman. You

just need her mother's permission, which means that the power in the courtship process lies with women. Fathers still have a say in who their daughter ultimately marries, but the decision about who can pursue her during the courtship process is in the hands of mothers and daughters. And although mothers and fathers certainly consider the economic prospects of their daughter's suitor, the process of courtship itself is not an economic transaction.

If you navigate the system of calling successfully, you'll hopefully end up married. But exactly what type of marriage will it be?

↗ You end up in a companionate marriage. **GO TO 109.**

↖ You end up in a traditional marriage. **GO TO 110.**

↘ You don't get married. **GO TO 105.**

123

You're in a culture where dating is the predominant mode of courtship, so you might find yourself going out on a date. Dating first evolved as a courtship method in the early twentieth century. It started partly because of a lack of space. The previous system of courtship—calling—required some space in a house where a young woman and her suitor could hang out, under adult supervision. But what if you didn't have a house to hang out in? Working-class women had already begun dating—leaving their home in the company of a male suitor without the supervision of an adult chaperone. When even middle-class women started moving out of their parents' houses to go work in cities, they were usually stuck without a space in which to entertain male suitors and without any adult supervision. Dating began to make more sense.

Dating then meant that, as a young woman, you waited for a man to ask you out on a date and then went out somewhere with your suitor. This is often still the case today. The man often decides where you go on the date and pays for whatever your dating activities cost. A dating system turns courtship into an economic exchange, something that our nineteenth-century ancestors, who were raised under the calling system of courtship, would find horrifying. Because men do the asking, the planning, and the paying, the power in this courtship system is firmly in their hands.

Courtship is still around as a system as dating today. You might follow the rules as laid out above. Or, as a young woman, you might be the person who does the asking instead of the person who waits to be asked. You might split the costs for the date evenly, lessening the power imbalance of this particular courtship system.

If you successfully navigate the rules of dating, you'll hopefully end up married. Or maybe not. If you do, what kind of marriage will you find yourself in?

- ↗ You end up in a companionate marriage. **GO TO 109.**
- ↖ You end up in a traditional marriage. **GO TO 110.**
- ↘ You don't get married. **GO TO 105.**

124

You live in a time and place where hookups have become an accepted form of sexual and romantic interaction, which means that you're probably in the United States on a college campus, where hookup culture is most commonly found. You might not be sure whether hookups are a form of courtship or just a recreational activity, and you're not alone. Because hookups are a relatively new phenomenon, the extent to which they may lead to serious, committed relationships isn't clear.

In fact, there's some debate about what exactly the term *hookup* means. A hookup is generally seen as a one-time sexual encounter that carries no further expectations or obligations. In theory, a hookup is generally not seen as a first date or a pathway to a more committed relationship. For some people, a hookup specifically involves sex, but for other people, it can mean kissing or making out or any variety of sexual activity. On your particular college campus, it might feel like everyone is hooking up, even if you aren't hooking up yourself. In fact, research shows that although not many college students actually engage in hookups, they assume that everyone else is doing

it. So hooking up does dominate the sexual and romantic terrain of many college campuses, even though it's not what most
people are doing.

You might view hookups as a form of sexual convergence,
or the way in which norms regarding sexuality for women
and men have become more similar over time. If your mom
or grandma went to college, they probably would've thought
that the idea of hooking up with a guy on campus was pretty
strange. Women's sexuality was much more restricted in the
past, which meant that a woman openly pursuing an encounter
that was about nothing other than sexual pleasure would have
been frowned on. With sexual convergence, it's increasingly
acceptable for women to act like men in their sexual lives. You
might see hookups as a reflection of that trend.

Interestingly, this hookup culture so far hasn't resulted in
college students today having more sex with more partners
than previous generations did. When researchers ask about
the frequency of sex and number of sexual partners, the
numbers are about the same as they were for their parents'
generation. Sometimes, hookups do evolve into committed
relationships. You might transition from hooking up to being
friends with benefits, and then, eventually, to being in an
exclusive relationship.

Why have hookups become an important mode of sexual
and romantic interaction on college campuses? Some speculate

that it's because of the sped-up, hyperinvolved lifestyle of today's middle-class young adults. If you're constantly on the go with schoolwork and extracurricular activities, you might not have time to date. But you still want some sexual activity, so hookups are an efficient solution.

Others have speculated that hookup culture is connected to the growing gender imbalance on college campuses. Most colleges and universities struggle to maintain a balanced gender ratio, because women are outperforming men academically and are therefore more likely to be admitted to college. It's not at all uncommon to find campuses with three-to-two or two-to-one ratios skewed toward women. When men are outnumbered by women, men have more power to set the terms of heterosexual courtship and relationships, since heterosexual women are competing for a limited number of heterosexual men. College men dictate a system that meets their needs— casual, obligation-free sexual encounters.

The truth is that hookup culture doesn't mean that most young people won't end up married. If you do end up walking down the aisle, what exactly will that marriage look like?

↗ You end up in a companionate marriage. **GO TO 109.**

↖ You end up in a traditional marriage. **GO TO 110.**

↘ You don't get married. **GO TO 105.**

125

For most of the history of the United States, women of color and white, working-class women have worked outside the home. The popular narrative that women first started getting jobs in large numbers in the 1960s and '70s, as a result of the women's movement, really only applies to the small number of (usually white) women who were able to afford to be stay-at-home mothers in the first place.

If you're an African American woman, you've inherited the legacy of slavery; your ancestors most likely spent long periods of history subjected to forced, unpaid labor. After the worldwide abolition of chattel slavery and emancipation in the United States, African American women still usually worked, and though they were paid, it wasn't much. Other women of color and working-class white women historically almost always worked for pay, and they also weren't paid very well.

The idea of the nuclear family, made up of a father who goes to work and a mother who stays home and takes care of the kids, has always been less accessible for women of color and working-class white women like you. Today, thanks in part to factors like inflation and wage stagnation, having one potential breadwinner stay home is a luxury that the majority of U.S. families—of all races and ethnicities—can't afford.

↖ **GO TO 143.**

126

As a white, middle- or upper-class woman, working outside the home might be a decision for you instead of a necessity. Your partner might make enough money to make your income optional, and, if so, you're in a minority of today's families in the United States.

Women like you—and especially women with children—began to enter the workforce in growing numbers in the 1960s and '70s. Women began working partly because of the increasing independence that the women's movement brought. That emphasis on independence and women's empowerment made working outside the home much more attractive to you than it might have been in the past, pulling you into work. But you would've been pushed into the workforce as much as you were pulled. Another reason that more middle- and upper-class women began working was because of the decline in the real value of men's wages. In other words, you were pushed into the workplace in order to help your family survive. This is called wage stagnation, and it happens when incomes don't keep up with inflation, so that over time, people are effectively getting paid less and less. Some estimates suggest that, when adjusted for inflation, the median male, full-time worker in 1973 earned almost $3,000 more than his counterpart in 2014 ($53,294 in 1973 compared to $50,383 in 2014). Since 1970, men's wages have decreased 19 percent due to wage stagnation. That means that even for white, middle- and upper-class women like you, surviving on one income is becoming increasingly impossible.

↖ **GO TO 143.**

127

As a woman who doesn't work for pay outside the home, you probably still do work—and possibly much more of it than men. In fact, estimates tell us that when we include unpaid work—like household chores and caring for children—women work longer hours than men. In developed countries, women work thirty minutes longer per day, while in developing country, you'll work fifty minutes longer on average than men. Much of your work will take the form of housework and childcare. Even though the hours that you spend cooking or taking care of children are crucial to the household and allow your spouse the freedom to go earn wages, this type of work is viewed as something that you're simply expected to do. The world's economy couldn't function without the unpaid labor of women like you, but when most people think of "work," they generally don't think of the unpaid labor performed by women. The idea of work itself is deeply gendered.

↖ **GO TO 144.**

128

If you're a man who does no paid work, you're pretty rare. Working for pay, and usually doing so outside the home, is central to how masculinity is defined. Part of what it means to be a man is to be able to support your family financially. That means that you're much less likely than women to do only unpaid work. Only 7 percent of fathers who live with their children are stay-at-home dads.

Why don't more guys like you decide to give up the workplace in exchange for the hard work of taking care of a home and raising children? One answer might be the financial costs. Because men make more than women on average in just about every country in the world, it makes more sense, if you're a heterosexual couple, for the woman to give up her salary and stay home—it's usually easier to support a family on a man's salary alone than it would be with a woman's income alone.

But money doesn't appear to be the only reason that you're less likely to become a stay-at-home dad. In many Scandinavian countries, generous parental paid leave is available to both mothers and fathers. Unlike in the United States, paid leave in these countries is mandated by the government, rather than left up to individual employers. This paid leave reduces the financial costs to families when men stay home, yet men still don't take advantage of it to the same extent that women do.

Take Sweden as an example. Sweden introduced a paid parental leave program for fathers forty years ago, but in the first year of the program, men took less than 1 percent of all paid parental leave. The Swedish government turned the tide when they added yet another financial incentive to the program. The "daddy month" gave couples an extra month of paid leave if both parents took at least one month of leave. With this change, the proportion of men taking paid leave jumped significantly. In 2016, the program was expanded to give three extra months of paid leave. Today, men take about 25 percent of all parental leave, and Sweden is still working to make parental leave even more equal. Other countries that have tried similar policies have seen comparable results. Two years after adding similar incentives to its paid leave program, Germany saw the rate of men taking parental leave rise from 3 percent to more than 20 percent.

There are rewards for you as a dad for spending more time with your children, and it's good for women too. In Sweden, women's income and their reported levels of happiness have both increased as more men take advantage of parental leave.

Outside of countries like Sweden and Germany, you're less

likely to be doing no paid work at all. You'll probably still help out with housework and childcare, since in two-thirds of U.S. families, both mom and dad work. But you'll probably spend less time doing this unpaid work. On average, fathers in the United States spend seven hours a week on childcare, nine hours on housework, and forty-three hours doing paid work. Mothers spend on average fifteen hours a week on childcare, eighteen hours on housework, and twenty-five hours on paid work.

↖ **GO TO 144.**

129

As a man, paid work is kind of your thing. The world is divided in such a way that men are assumed to be the ones who do paid work, even if it hasn't always been that way. The doctrine of separate spheres—or the idea that men belong at work and women's place is in the home—has really only been around for about two hundred years. Before that, all work was done at home and usually on a farm. That's why the word *housework* didn't become commonplace until the 1800s. Before that, all work was housework, or work done in the home by both women and men, as well as their children.

> **SEPARATE SPHERES DOCTRINE**
>
> *n.* /ˈse-p(ə-)rət ˈsfirs ˈdäk-trən/
>
> The idea that men belong at work, and a woman's place is in the home.

That paid work came to be defined as masculine has all kinds of implications for you as a man in the workplace today. Since the doctrine of separate spheres, workplaces have been largely masculine spaces, designed for men and assumed to be occupied mostly by men. You can see this in the fact that it wasn't until the 1970s that employers began to develop any sort of sexual harassment policies for the workplace. Before that, the workplace was just assumed to be hostile toward women because it was a masculine space, not for women.

The idea of a family wage is another way in which work is shaped by gender. The family wage is the basic idea that an employee should be paid enough to support a family. That might not seem to have anything to do with gender, until you think about who's generally expected to be the person support-ing a family—men. The idea that men need an income large enough to support a family contributes in subtle and not-so-subtle ways to the gender pay gap. Employers generally don't assume that a woman needs to be paid enough to support a family, even though 42 percent of households with children in the United States are headed by women. In the past, employ-ers would explicitly refuse to hire or promote women, because they believed that this would mean taking jobs away from men and the families who needed their support.

Partly because of this belief in men as breadwinners, having children will help you in your career in ways that it won't help women. Your female counterparts will experience a "mother-hood penalty"—they'll make less money over the course of their careers if they have children. But there's no fatherhood penalty for you. In fact, men with children make more money than men without children. This is due in part to the assumption, conscious or not, that men are the breadwinners for their family. Men need to be paid enough to support a family while women do not.

↖ **GO TO 144.**

130

You were born a biological woman but are living as a man. Transgender people like you experience discrimination, harassment, and violence in a wide variety of settings. Trans men may be fired outright from their jobs. Or your employer or fellow employees may act in subtler ways that make your workplace hostile and uncomfortable until you quit. If, for example, as a woman, you worked in the front end of a business, interacting with customers, your employer may move you to the back during or after your transition. Federal laws about discrimination in the workplace don't explicitly cover transgender individuals like you, so the options available to you for fighting this kind of treatment are limited.

Under certain circumstances in the workplace, however, you might be accepted as "just one of the guys" and find yourself able to take advantage of some of the privileges that come with masculinity. Some trans men report that after their transition from women to men, they have access to more authority; are seen as more competent; receive more respect and recognition; and find more economic opportunities available to them. In other words, as a trans man, you might be able to cash in on the patriarchal dividend, or the unearned benefits that come with conforming to masculinity. This will be even more likely if you're stealthy, meaning that you don't reveal your transgender identity to your coworkers. You'll be most likely to benefit from the patriarchal dividend if you fit prescribed notions of masculinity—if you're tall, white, and successfully able to pass as a man.

If you remain employed at the same company throughout your transition, you might find that clients or coworkers who are unaware of your transition might actually point out how much better you are relative to your former, feminine self. In one example of this dynamic, a woman named Susan worked as an attorney at the same law firm throughout her transition to living as a man named Thomas. Before the transition, a male colleague had recommended that Susan be fired for being "incompetent." After the transition, that same colleague was pleased to find that Susan had been replaced by a new guy, Thomas, who he praised as "just delightful"—never realizing that Susan and Thomas were the same person. So as a trans man, you might go from being incompetent to delightful when all you've changed is your gender.

↖ **GO TO 144.**

131

Gender and sexuality aren't connected in your culture. That means that the ways of making sense of sexuality have to do with something besides who has what genitalia or who acts more feminine or masculine. How could that possibly work?

What if instead of choosing our sexual partners based on gender, which doesn't always result in the best sexual compatibility, we all wore colored bracelets that expressed our particular set of likes and dislikes? A yellow bracelet on your left wrist might indicate that you really like performing oral sex, while a yellow bracelet on your right wrist would mean that you like receiving oral sex. A green bracelet would mean you're really into feet, while a purple bracelet might mean you like superhero role-playing. That's one way potential way of organizing sexuality that has nothing to do with gender.

In ancient Greek culture, people might not have worn sex bracelets, but sex was about more than just gender. Among the ancient Greeks, men regularly had sex with other men. But it wouldn't make sense to call this behavior homosexuality, partly because that word didn't exist back then. It also wouldn't make sense to call it homosexuality because for the ancient Greeks, same-gender sexual behaviors didn't have the same meaning. The word *homosexuality* carries with it all the particular beliefs that are assumed in contemporary Anglo-European culture. For example, we believe that you have to be either homosexual or heterosexual—you can't be both at the same time. And we assume that being homosexual is an essential part of your identity, tied to your biology or your psychology.

The ancient Greeks didn't associate any of these things with same-gender sexual behavior, so they weren't really talking about homosexuality at all. In ancient Greece, what was most important was that sex maintain the established social hierarchy, or the ranking of different groups. That meant that it was perfectly okay for men who were Greek citizens to have sex with their male slaves, as long as they were the dominant partner. It was also okay for male Greek citizens to have sex with women as the dominant partner. It wouldn't be okay for a male slave to be the dominant partner with a male Greek citizen. In this particular way of viewing sexual behavior, gender wasn't the most important factor for determining what was considered "right" and "wrong" or "normal" and "abnormal." Correct sexual behavior was behavior that followed the lines of power, which didn't necessarily overlap with gender.

Power is one alternative way of organizing sexuality, but it's just one among many other possibilities.

↖ To explore a different gender path, **TURN BACK TO 2.**

132

You're an African American man, and there are many ways in which being African American intersects with your masculinity. For example, from a young age, the behavior of white boys is often justified with phrases like "boys will be boys." This understanding of masculinity excuses the behavior of white boys and men as something both essential to their identity and beyond their control. It can be used to explain boys being rowdy, but also boys being violent or aggressive toward each other or toward girls.

Research tells us that in schools, teachers often don't apply this kind of explanation to the behavior of African American boys. Their behaviors are not seen as excusable, but as a sign of their violent or aggressive nature. In this way, the behavior of African American boys is seen as both more dangerous and more adult. In part, this helps explain why so many African American boys and men become the victims of unjust police violence. Your actions as an African American boy are understood through a much different lens than those of boys of different racial backgrounds. Your race intersects with your gender to shape your experiences in important ways.

In the workplace, you won't share in many of the privileges that white men have due to their race and gender. For example, research tells us that in female-dominated occupations, white men experience a glass escalator. If you're the only white male librarian, you're likely to get pushed toward administrative positions with more authority and better pay. This isn't true of African American men in predominantly female occupations. Unlike your white male counterparts, your coworkers, both male and female, will not embrace you and encourage you in ways that make the glass escalator a reality.

↖ **GO TO 113.**

133

You're an African American woman, and your race, gender, and sexual identity all intersect in important ways. An intersectional approach helps us see how gender and sexuality are often used to construct the boundaries between different racial and ethnic groups. One way to argue that a certain racial or ethnic group is inferior is to point to how their ideas about gender or sexuality are different and, usually, somehow worse than your own. Often this means suggesting that a racial or ethnic group is more sexual than yours.

From the very beginning of encounters between Europeans and African peoples, sexuality was used to draw distinctions.

INTERSECTIONAL

adj. / ˌin-tər-ˈsek-shnəl/

Relating to the complex way in which the effects of multiple forms of discrimination—such as racism, sexism, and classism—combine, especially in the experiences of marginalized individuals or groups.

Early depictions of African women exaggerated the size of their breasts and genitalia and almost always depicted them naked, in order to encourage the view of African women as hypersexual. This hypersexuality

↙   →

was then contrasted with the purity of white, European women and used as evidence in support of arguments about the inferiority of African peoples. Depictions equating dark-skinned women with animals were also common. You can still see this in advertising images today, where many African American women are depicted wearing animal prints or in exotic, "primitive" settings.

This imagery has real effects on how you'll be treated as an African American woman. Research shows that the behaviors of African American girls in school are more likely to be seen as sexualized relative to girls of other racial backgrounds. As an African American girl, you're also more likely to be seen as overly aggressive, domineering, and unfeminine.

When you do stand up for what you believe in as an African American woman, your voice is likely to go unheard. Women like you have often been at the forefront of important social movements like feminism and the civil rights movement, but your role is often downplayed or ignored. Most recently, the Black Lives Matter movement was started by three African American women. From the first wave of the women's movement into the twenty-first century, you have to work extra hard as an African American woman to make sure your viewpoint is included.

↖ **GO TO 113.**

↑ ↗

134

You're a Latinx woman and that can mean a lot of things. The experiences of Latinx people are as diverse as the experiences of people in any racial and ethnic group. But when you're a woman of color, much of that diversity of experience gets erased by stereotypes. Stereotypes of Latinx people as illegal immigrants might affect how people interact with you, even if your family has been in the United States for generations or since the very beginning. Especially in today's atmosphere of increasing hostility toward immigrants, you might face violence, intimidation, and discrimination.

Other stereotypes will focus on your sexuality. Research tells us that in some sex education classes in high schools, Latinx girls are assumed to already be sexually knowledgeable and sexually active in a way that is not true of their white counterparts. Teachers might assume that, as a Latinx girl, you have a higher risk of teen pregnancy and attribute this risk to aspects of Latinx culture. Your race intersects with your gender to shape your experiences in important ways.

↖ **GO TO 113.**

↙ →

135

You're a Latinx man. Like African American boys, your behaviors as a child in school are less likely to be excused as just "boys being boys" than they would be if you were a white boy. As a Latinx boy, your rowdy or physical behaviors are not seen as excusable, but as a reflection of machismo, or an emphasis on men and male power that is supposed to be part of Latinx culture. In this way, your behavior as a Latinx boy is seen as both beyond your control and a natural result of your cultural background.

This idea of machismo may be reinforced by the way men like you are depicted in the media. Latinx men in TV and film are most likely to be portrayed as drug dealers, gang members, or other types of criminals. Even if Latinx men aren't depicted as out-and-out criminals, they're likely to be characterized as illegal immigrants. This might

---

XENOPHOBIA

n. / ˌze-nə-ˈfō-bē-ə, ˌzē-/

Fear and hatred of strangers, outsiders, or people foreign to the aggressor's culture.

---

mean that even if your family has been in the United States for generations, people will still think of you as a new arrival.

In an increasingly xenophobic atmosphere (a culture charac-terized by hostility toward outsiders), you may find yourself the victim of violence, intimidation, and discrimination. Your actions as a Latinx man are understood through a much dif-ferent lens than those of men of different racial backgrounds. Your race intersects with your gender to shape your experi-ences in important ways.

↖ **GO TO 113.**

136

As an Asian American man, you're likely to be subjected to the model minority myth. That is, people will be likely to believe that you're smart, especially when it comes to subjects like math. When you're in school, they might ask you for help with homework and not believe you if you tell them that you don't know the answers. People will hold you and other Asian Americans up as an example to other racial groups as a model of success. They might ask, "Why can't African American people do was well as Asian Americans?" Because many people believe that Asian Americans have achieved success in the United States, they're likely to ignore or discount the experiences of more recent Asian American immigrants, who continue to face discrimination and blocked access to economic opportunities.

Compared to men of other racial and ethnic groups, you might be seen as less masculine. The images of Asian American men that you see in the media often portray you as nerdy and asexual, although this is a shift from the past. During World War II, you would have been perceived as part of the "yellow menace" or "yellow peril" especially if you were Japanese

American, but also if you were Chinese American or Korean American. Propaganda from this period depicted Japanese men as animal-like potential rapists, waiting to attack white women. If you were Japanese American during this period, you were likely to be interred in camps and seen as the enemy. The contemporary legacy of this long history of discrimination is that you might be treated as not quite fully American.

↖ **GO TO 113.**

137

You're an Asian American woman. Research suggests that you're more likely than women of other races and ethnicities to be seen as passive, weak, excessively submissive, and sexually exotic. The images you see of yourself in the media will likely reinforce these ideas. Asian American women are often depicted as prostitutes or victims of sex trafficking. Like your male counterparts, people might also expect you to be smarter and more successful, as part of the model minority myth.

If you're an Asian American mother, you might be subjected to a newer stereotype—that of the tiger mother. This stereotype depicts Asian American mothers as strict and demanding, ruthlessly pushing their children toward academic success and often veering into potentially abusive behavior. The tiger mother can be seen as a variation of another stereotype of Asian American women: the dragon lady. The dragon lady is aggressive and opportunistic, usually using sexuality to get what she wants. Both of these stereotypes use gender to draw a boundary between Asian Americans and other groups by portraying Asian American women as aggressive and domineering—a reversal of how gender roles are supposed to be and therefore a sign of your inferiority as a group.

↖ **GO TO 113.**

138

You're an Arab American man. In part because of the way that Arab American men are portrayed in the media, you'll have to deal with the stereotype of Arab American men as terrorists. In the United States, you may be subject to violence and harassment because of your racial and ethnic background. You'll find it difficult to travel in and out of the country, getting pulled aside when you go through airport security even when you're an American citizen.

As far as gender goes, people might believe that you're sexist or oppressive toward women, based on their incorrect assumptions about gender relations in Arab countries. This stereotype is a way in which gender is used to draw distinctions between different groups: those seeking to establish the inferiority of Arab Americans as a group will use this stereotype as evidence for their argument.

↖ **GO TO 113.**

139

You're an Arab American woman. In today's world, you're likely to encounter discrimination and suspicion based on your racial and ethnic background and the incorrect belief that Arab Americans are terrorists. This will be true even though many more people in the United States have died at the hands of white men than have been killed by Arab people.

If you're also Muslim (not all Arab Americans are Muslim and not all Muslims are Arab American) and you wear a hijab, people might believe that you're being oppressed by the men in your culture. Whatever form your hijab takes—a head scarf or a more extensive burka that covers your face too—you might face discrimination and hostility due to your style of dress. The meaning that hijab holds for you will probably be very different from the meaning that is assumed by other people. You may wear hijab as a sign of your deep faith or to demonstrate connection to your family, community, and country. You may feel that, rather than being a sign of your oppression as a woman, hijab is a symbol of your empowerment. In hijab, you can escape the objectification that comes from men looking at your body. You feel that hijab allows you to interact with men based on who you are, rather than what you look like. You might point out that other women are the ones who are truly oppressed by their need to appear beautiful and attractive all the time. These issues related to hijab are just one possible way in which your gender might interact with your identity as an Arab American woman.

↖ **GO TO 113.**

140

You're a white man. You move through life as both white and masculine, even if as a white person you don't spend a lot of time thinking about your race. The ability to not have to think too much about how your whiteness impacts your day-to-day life is one of the privileges, or benefits that you did nothing to get, that go along with your identity. There's a lot of power that comes with being a white man in most places in the world.

In the United States, most of the representations of masculinity that you see are white representations. All but one of the forty-five presidents of the United States have been white men like you. Everywhere you look, you see men like you in positions of power. On average, you make more money than any other group in the United States. It might be easier for you, as a white man, to come close to the ideal forms of masculinity that are held up in your culture than it is for men from other racial and ethnic groups.

White men have it pretty good, but it might not feel that way to you, personally. There's a great irony that even though a lot of power is conferred on white men by the systems of race and gender in which we live, many white men don't feel particularly powerful. Why is that? Part of the answer has to do with how difficult it is to make connections between our individual lives and larger social structures. When you go through your day-to-day life as a white man, the power that you have isn't obvious because it's something that you take for granted. You don't have to worry about being profiled based on your race, so you're less likely to be pulled over in your car by the police or pulled out of the line at airport security. Compared to women, people assume that you have knowledge and authority. They'll defer to you in conversations and ask you for help, even when the issue or task at hand isn't something that you particularly know about or can do. If you want to return an item at a store, no one will question you. No one will follow you around when you're shopping, assuming that you're going to steal something. You'll find it easier to get a loan, to buy a car or a house, or start your own business.

All of these things are true, but if you have no sense of how other people have to deal with challenges like these every day, you might focus instead on the ways in which you don't have power. You might focus instead on the fact that you can no longer tell sexual jokes in the workplace, for fear of accusations of sexual harassment. Or the fact that when you call an automated phone service, you have to listen to a prompt for instructions in Spanish. Very small changes like these may stick out to you without any connection to the many, many ways in which you still have power. Without any awareness of the big power that you have as a white man, these very small changes can seem magnified.

↖ **GO TO 113.**

141

You're a white woman. Even if, as a white person, you don't spend a lot of time thinking about your race, it matters for how you experience your gender. The ability to not have to think too much about how your whiteness impacts your day-to-day life is one of the privileges, or benefits that you did nothing to get, that go along with your identity.

As a white woman, you can assume that when people talk about "women's issues," they're probably talking about your issues specifically. For much of its history, feminism has been dominated by other white women like you. From the very beginnings of the women's movement in the United States, women of color were involved and in the front lines. But their particular needs and interests were often pushed to the side. In a famous speech, Sojourner Truth pointed out the differences between the experiences of many white women and her experience as a freed slave. Unlike white women, Truth was never treated as delicate and therefore incapable of working. She was never put up on a pedestal. Like many women of color throughout U.S. history, Truth always worked.

That your experiences as a white woman are seen as the norm is an important way in which your race and gender intersect. That doesn't mean that you don't face discrimination as a woman, based on your gender. But power and privilege are complicated things, and though you may be oppressed as a woman, your whiteness also gives you power.

↖ **GO TO 113.**

142

You were born a biological man and are living as a woman. Transgender people like you experience discrimination, harassment, and violence in a wide variety of settings. Trans women may be fired outright from their jobs. Or your employer or fellow employees may act in subtler ways that make your workplace hostile and uncomfortable until you quit.

Because the workplace is a masculine space, you're likely to face a great deal of discrimination and harassment if you transition during your working life. As a trans woman, you might be fired from your job after your transition. You'll also experience a decrease in your earnings as a woman relative to what you made or would've made living as a man. Philecia Barnes served as an Ohio police officer for twenty years (as a man) and scored in the top 20 percent on her sergeant exam. But when she began her transition and started to look feminine, she was demoted rather than promoted. Federal laws about discrimination in the workplace don't explicitly cover transgender individuals like you, so the options available to you for fighting this kinds of treatment are limited. Like Philecia, you're likely to lose your patriarchal dividend in the workplace as a trans woman.

↖ **GO TO 144.**

143

You're one of the increasing numbers of women worldwide who work for pay outside the home, in addition to the work you do inside the household. Chances are, you'll get paid less than your male counterparts for the work that you do. As a woman in the United States, you're likely to earn 80 cents for every dollar earned by men. That's the average, but the gender pay gap will be much worse if you're a woman of color. For example, if you're a Latinx woman, you'll make 54 cents for every dollar earned by white men. If you're an African American woman, you'll earn 63 cents for every white man's dollar.

Why are you, as a woman, earning less than most men? There are lots of factors that we know go into explaining the gender pay gap, as well as some unknowns. One of the first things to consider is whether or not you're working in a job with a high level of gender segregation. Is almost everyone in the place where you work of the same gender, or is there a pretty even distribution across genders?

↗ You work in a place with high gender segregation. **GO TO 151.**

↘ You work in a place with low gender segregation. **GO TO 152.**

144

You probably don't spend all your time working. Everyone needs to relax and have a little fun from time to time. But even in your spare time, you won't completely escape the effects of gender.

- ↗ You're a woman (a cis woman or a trans woman). **GO TO 156.**
- ↘ You're a man (a cis man or a trans man). **GO TO 157.**

145

Different sorts of jobs require different sorts of skills. Working in a factory might require physical dexterity or strength. As a woman, you're likely to find yourself working in a job that requires emotional labor. Emotional labor is work that requires you to either induce or suppress feelings, in order to produce a certain state of mind in other people—usually customers or clients. In other words, emotional labor means that your job requires you to hide the fact that you're angry or sad or bored so that you can keep the customer happy. Think of the emotional labor a waitress does. If her customers make her angry or disgusted, she can't let that show. She has to continue to act polite, pleasant, and cheerful, in order to keep the people she's waiting on happy. It is, in fact, part of her job description to keep her customers happy.

Most service jobs like waiting tables involve emotional labor. And not surprisingly, women dominate service jobs. But emotional labor isn't valued as highly as other types of skills and abilities, so women in service jobs generally make less than men in other types of occupations. Take the example of paralegals, a profession that emerged in the 1960s. Eighty-five percent of paralegals are women. They do many of the same tasks as the lawyers they assist but get paid much less. Lawyers, only 36 percent of whom are women, earn more than twice as much as their paralegal counterparts. Paralegals' regular duties include doing legal research, summarizing court transcripts and depositions, and reviewing and analyzing documents produced in large litigation cases. None of these are tasks that lawyers themselves don't also do. The main difference between a paralegal and a lawyer is the emotional labor required of paralegals, who are expected to nurture and mother their bosses.

↖ **GO TO 144.**

146

If you play any kind of sport at almost any level, you probably play in a gender-segregated setting. That is, if you're a woman, you play sports with and against other women. If you're a man, you play with and against other men. You can count on one hand the number of competitive sports that aren't gender-segregated—horse racing, automobile racing, and ultimate Frisbee. Here's a question you've probably never asked yourself: Why are sports segregated by gender? Does it make sense to organize sports this way? The answer is yes, if part of the purpose of sports is to reinforce gender differences, which is exactly what sports in their current configuration do.

For much of the early history of organized sports, women were excluded from competing. In fact, even cheerleading as a sport used to be just for guys. Women didn't take over cheerleading until after World War II. Excluding women from sports obviously helped contribute to beliefs about gender differences. Women were said to be too delicate for the exertion and physical contact that came with playing sports. In fact, playing sports was often specifically about increasing and reinforcing masculinity, and women weren't supposed to have any part in that. During the early twentieth century, President Theodore Roosevelt worried that with the closing of the American frontier and the rise of office jobs, American men would lose their rugged masculinity. He very intentionally promoted the sport of American football as a solution to his worries about the loss of masculinity. When women did start to play sports, their participation was limited to certain activities that were considered appropriately feminine. Namely, women weren't supposed to sweat or engage in physical contact.

Women in the United States began entering sports in unprecedented numbers in the wake of the passage of Title IX in 1972. This piece of legislation dictated that any colleges and universities that received federal funding (which is pretty much all colleges and universities) had to provide equal opportunities for women and men. As it applied to sports, that meant that colleges needed to provide equal opportunities for their male and female students to receive athletic scholarships and play sports. In the decades since Title IX, the participation of girls and women in a wide variety of sports has increased dramatically at all levels. But women and men by and large still play sports separately. Teams are generally gender integrated only when there aren't high enough numbers of children to make up gender-segregated teams.

Arguments in favor of gender segregation in sports are

usually based on presumed differences in athletic ability between men and women. But differences in athletic ability are based on more than just anatomy and are shaped by social forces, as well. For example, in almost all types of races at the elite athletic level, women's times have been converging with men's over the past century. Women athletes are getting faster and faster. Why? In part, it's because with increased gender equality, elite sports programs across the globe are distributing their resources between men and women athletes more equitably. Women are getting more and better resources, equipment, and attention than they did in the past. The question of whether women's athletic performance will catch up with men's remains unanswered. But part of that answer lies in the motivation for women to pursue athletics at the elite level.

Are the rewards for female and male athletes still unequal? The answer is a resounding yes. Tennis is one of the few sports where women are compensated at the same level as their male counterparts, and it took decades of struggle to obtain that equality. It's only recently that elite tennis tournaments began to pay men and women the same, after a battle that began with Billie Jean King in the 1970s and ended with Venus and Serena Williams finally achieving the goal of equity in major tournament prizes in the 2000s (although pay disparity often still happens in smaller tournaments). In every other professional sport, women are paid less than men, even if their sport is more popular and successful. The U.S. women's national soccer team, despite having won three World Cup championships, is still paid less than the men's team, which has won zero World Cup titles. In 2017, Sylvia Fowles, the highest-paid WNBA player, made a mere $109,000 compared to the $37.4 million made by Steph Curry, the NBA's highest-paid player, in the 2017–2018 season. Women playing professional softball in the United States make between $5,000 and $6,000 for the season. That's compared to the average salary of $4.5 million for a Major League Baseball player. We live in a society where monetary rewards are at least part of what motivates our behavior. So, we can assume that these salaries, which aren't even enough to live on, might affect the amount of time, effort, and resources women dedicate to becoming an elite athlete in their sport. The fact is that most women won't be able to earn a living playing their sport at the professional level.

We don't know for sure exactly how close we might get to closing the gap in athletic performance between women and men. Given today's differences, how could sports be reorganized in a way that's not gender segregated? One possibility would be to structure leagues on the basis of athletic ability, rather than on gender. There's precedent for this in sports like wrestling and boxing, which use weight classes for matching competitors. In this system, instead of separate men's and women's basketball leagues, there would be different levels of ability-based leagues, similar to what exists in Major League Baseball, with A, double-A, and triple-A levels. Instead of assuming that gender automatically divides people by their skills and abilities, these leagues would use individuals' actual, demonstrated skills and abilities to structure competition.

↗ You play Olympic sports. **GO TO 153.**

↘ You don't play Olympic sports. **GO TO 147.**

147

Even if you're not necessarily the sporty type, your body will still matter for how you experience gender. Being a man or a woman will make a difference in terms of what types of illnesses you experience, as well as what happens when you get ill. Gender also plays a role in how long you're likely to live and how you'll die.

↗ You're a man. **GO TO 158.**

→ You're a woman. **GO TO 159.**

↘ You're a transgender person. **GO TO 160.**

148

The way you live your gender continues to shift and change throughout your life, so there really isn't an end to your gender adventure. Hopefully at this point you have a better understanding of the ways in which gender in all its complexity unfolds in our lives. You're ready to contemplate a final question: Is gender a category that we should be working to get rid of, or not?

- ↗ You think gender should stay the same as it is now. **GO TO 95.**
- → You think we should work for more gender equality. **GO TO 100.**
- ↖ You think we should work to get rid of gender altogether. **GO TO 108.**
- ↘ You have a completely new and different idea about what should happen to gender in the future. **GO TO 161.**

149

Your experience as a woman going to the doctor will be shaped by your gender in important ways. This is partly because of the long and complicated history between women and medicine as an institution. Doctors have a long history of both ignoring women's unique medical problems and simultaneously treating women's bodies as inherently diseased. Take the case of hysteria, a disease commonly diagnosed among women in the nineteenth century. Hysteria was literally defined as a disease of the womb. The symptoms included nervousness, emotional outbursts, and hallucinations.

Hysteria was an especially common diagnosis among upper-class women; writers like Virginia Woolf and Charlotte Perkins Gilman were both diagnosed with hysteria. There were a variety of treatments for hysteria. The rest cure dictated that women be isolated from all activities and forced to stay in bed for extended periods of time. Inducing an orgasm was used as another method of treatment, and doctors treated women with medical devices that were the first vibrators. Hysteria is no longer seen as a real disease, and many historians understand its existence as an attempt to control the activities of creative and powerful women.

Hysteria is an example of the medical institution turning the basic functions of a woman's body (having a womb) into a disease. In other cases, the differences between women's and men's bodies have been ignored in ways that are harmful to women. For example, women on average have a higher percentage of fat deposits in their bodies, which affects the absorption of many types of drugs. It also turns out that the classic symptoms of a heart attack that have been broadcast for years don't apply exactly the same way where women are concerned. Women may experience chest pain or pain in their arms, but they're also more likely to experience other symptoms, like nausea, shortness of breath, or light-headedness. Because of these subtle differences, women are less likely to realize that they're having a heart attack and therefore less likely to call for emergency assistance.

There are also gender differences in how doctors react to reports of pain. If, as a woman, you tell your doctor that you're experiencing pain, your symptoms are more likely to be dismissed as emotional or psychogenic. In other words, doctors are more likely to assume that your pain isn't real. Not surprisingly, then, doctors don't treat your pain symptoms as aggressively as they would if you were a man. Or they might treat you for a mental health condition that you don't actually have.

Even if your doctor takes your pain seriously, she or he might be more likely to attribute it to gynecological problems. This is especially true of abdominal pain, which often gets dismissed as connected to menstrual symptoms or other routine issues.

↖ **GO TO 148.**

150

As a woman in some times and places, your health may be put at risk by ideological and political debates about your body and reproduction. Your body and your health will be a battleground where these larger debates play out. Your access to medical technologies that allow you to have control over your own reproduction may be limited, depending on where you are. And depending on how your gender intersects with factors like race and social class, people in power might intervene further to control your ability to make decisions about your reproductive health.

- ↗ You're a woman who has been a victim of attempts to limit your fertility. **GO TO 114.**
- ↘ You're a woman who has faced barriers to obtaining access to birth control. **GO TO 115.**

151

You work in an occupation with high levels of gender segregation. You might be an engineer (12 percent women) or a social worker (82 percent women) or a librarian (84 percent women). Regardless of whether your occupation is mostly men or mostly women, you'll probably make less than the men who are doing the same job. As a social worker, you'll make 85 cents for every dollar that a man makes in the same occupation. As an engineer, you'll make 84 cents and as a librarian, 92 cents.

What's going on here? you might ask yourself. Why is it that high rates of gender segregation, even in cases where the job is occupied mostly by women, also mean that there's a gender pay gap?

Part of the explanation has to do with how women and men are segregated within occupational categories. Say you're a librarian. Most of the people you work with are women. When white men enter into female-dominated occupations, they're likely to experience something called the glass escalator. That means that they get pushed up into positions with higher authority and power, as well as larger salaries. Being one of the few men among women benefits men in a way that being one of the few women among men does not. As one of a few male librarians, both men and women in your occupation will expect you to be in charge. They'll pressure you to move up into administrative positions, and the men who already occupy positions of power will help you up. In fact, there might even be some stigma attached to you if you're a man who doesn't want to move up. So even if most librarians are women, the few men in that occupation will make more money because of the glass escalator.

Levels of gender segregation are connected to income inequality, because the segregation makes it easier to justify paying women less. It's hard to argue that a woman should be paid less than a man for doing the exact same job. It's not surprising, then, that women and men very rarely do the exact same job.

As a woman, you'll probably be paid less, and you're also likely to be expected to do different sorts of things in your job.

↖ **GO TO 145.**

152

You might find yourself in one of the occupations in the United States with relatively low levels of gender segregation. Maybe you're a pharmacist (60 percent women) or a veterinarian (63 percent women) or a bartender (56 percent women). These occupations come pretty close to being filled equally by women and men. But within these occupational categories, you'll probably still find that you make less compared to the men in that same occupation. As a woman pharmacist, you'll make on average 88 cents for every dollar made by a man in the same occupation. Veterinarians will make 78 cents and bartenders 71 cents.

What is happening here? you might ask yourself, as a woman working as a pharmacist, a vet, or a bartender. *Why am I making less in the same occupation?* Part of the answer has to do with gender segregation that only becomes apparent at a more detailed level of analysis.

The figures given above are based on census data that uses occupational categories. Census data is our best source of information about occupational segregation because it already exists—the government collects the data every year. But occupational categories are kind of general in nature, and they miss a lot of detail. Take the bartender example. You might be employed as a bartender in a dive bar in a small town in Indiana. Someone else might work as a bartender in a private country club in Manhattan. Both of you fit into the occupational category of bartender, but your jobs are very different. Not surprisingly, so are your incomes. Getting down to this level of detail is called job-level gender segregation, and this reveals even higher levels of gender segregation.

Now you can start to see why there might still be a gender pay gap in the occupation of bartending. Yes, there are about equal numbers of women and men working as bartenders, but men are more likely to get the high-paying jobs. They're more likely to work in upscale clubs, resorts, and restaurants, where they get paid more and also receive much better tips.

As a woman, you'll probably be paid less, and you're also likely to be expected to do different sorts of things in your job.

↖ **GO TO 145.**

153

If you're a woman and you have a body that's qualified to compete in the Olympics, you might be surprised to discover something new about your gender. Since the 1960s, the International Olympic Committee (IOC) has conducted gender testing on certain athletes. This practice began due to suspicions that certain countries were cheating by entering men to compete in women's sports.

Gender testing officially began to be used by the Olympic committee in the 1960s, and at first, it involved stripping women naked in order to examine their genitalia and other markers of biological gender. This came to be called the "nude parade," with women athletes lined up naked for examination. In other instances, women athletes were forced to lie on their backs with their knees raised for more detailed inspections. Obviously, this was a humiliating experience for female athletes. Partly due to complaints about these practices, the IOC shifted to a chromosome test in the late 1960s, which determined whether athletes had XX (female) or XY (male) chromosomes. Officials claimed that this would serve as a definitive test of athletes' underlying biological gender.

In some cases, this chromosome test revealed an underlying intersex condition of which athletes were previously unaware. A surprising number of women athletes were revealed to have chromosomes that didn't match either XX or XY, even though they had lived their whole lives as normal women. The IOC banned these women from competing, arguing that their intersex status gave them an unfair advantage due to increased levels of testosterone, which they suggested improves athletic ability. They maintained this position even though many of these women's intersex conditions meant that they were testosterone-resistant, meaning that they could not absorb testosterone even if there were high levels of the hormone present in their bodies.

Recently, women athletes have begun to challenge the practices of the IOC and other athletic governing bodies, like the International Association of Athletics Federations (IAAF), which governs track-and-field athletes. The IAAF revised its policy in 2011 to focus on "hyperandrogenism" instead of gender testing. Under this new policy, women whose testosterone levels were within the "male range" would be banned from competing as women. Exceptions would be made for women who were testosterone-resistant and women who reduced their testosterone levels below the "male range."

In the wake of this new policy, sports officials referred several women with higher testosterone levels to a clinic in France. There the women were advised to undergo surgery to have their internal testes removed, even though the organs posed no health threat to the young women. The surgeons also recommended removing their clitoris to make their external genitalia appear more "normal." The women, who were between the ages of 18 and 21, agreed to the surgeries; it's unclear whether anyone told them that the clitoral surgery would permanently reduce their sexual sensation.

A 2015 legal case ruled that the IAAF's testosterone-based policy is invalid, given the lack of scientific research demonstrating that testosterone provides any athletic advantage. The ruling gave the IAAF two years in which to gather evidence that testosterone does confer some advantage. As recently as March of 2018, the Court of Arbitration for Sports (CAS) gave the IAAF an additional six months to provide additional scientific evidence to support its testosterone-based policy.

You can imagine the trauma that you might experience as an Olympic-level female athlete suddenly being told that you're not really a woman and that you can't compete for an event you've trained for your whole life. You might also point out that all of this testing is directed only at women's athletics. It's assumed that there would be no advantage to a woman pretending to be a man, so men (including transgender men) aren't subjected to any of these tests. Transgender women who wish to compete in the Olympics must demonstrate that their testosterone levels have been below a certain cutoff point for at least a year prior to competition before they're allowed to participate.

↖ **GO TO 147.**

154

In the United States, the battle over women's access to birth control and other means of controlling their own reproductive lives has a long and contentious history. The struggle to give women access to birth control is ongoing and, in some ways, may be getting worse rather than better. This is true across a wide range of reproductive technologies.

Abortion is certainly the most controversial method of birth control in the United States. Although, technically, abortion has been legal in the United States since 1973, increasing numbers of restrictions on access to abortion have made it more difficult for women to make use of this often life-saving procedure. The number of abortion providers fell from a high in 1982 of 2,918 to 788 in 2014. These declines are due in large part to the organized campaign of violence against abortion providers. Eleven doctors and healthcare workers have been murdered by antiabortion activists, and seventeen have been the victims of attempted murders. This doesn't include bomb threats and other scare tactics used to terrorize abortion providers and the women who use these services.

Five states have only one abortion clinic serving the entire state population. That clinic may be hundreds of miles away from where you live and may only perform abortions one day a week. Many states have also instituted a mandatory waiting period. This means that you'll need to drive all the way to the clinic one day and then either rent a hotel room for the waiting period or drive back several days later. These logistics make abortion as good as impossible for women in many places across the United States.

You might find it difficult to access less controversial methods of birth control as well. Many insurance companies don't cover the cost of birth control. You may find yourself going to a drug store where the pharmacist refuses to fill birth control prescriptions based on their religious beliefs. If you're under the age of eighteen, you'll need parental permission to get access to most birth control. In general, getting access to Viagra, a drug to treat male impotence, will be much easier than getting birth control.

↖ **GO TO 148.**

155

On a global level, women's access to birth control varies a great deal. In the United States, access to all forms of birth control are becoming increasingly restricted. Not all insurance programs cover birth control (like pills, patches, shots, vaginal rings, and intrauterine devices), and a recent ruling by the Trump administration made it easier for employers to deny insurance coverage for birth control based on religious grounds. Low- and reduced-cost birth control is available through organizations like Planned Parenthood, but their government funding is continually being cut.

Compare this to places like the United Kingdom, where birth control is covered under the national healthcare program, making it affordable and accessible. Though getting an abortion in the United States is a cumbersome process, abortions in China are readily available and commonly used. On the other end of the spectrum, in countries like Ireland, the Dominican Republic, and El Salvador, abortion is illegal under most circumstances.

Ironically, if you're in a developing country experiencing

rapid population growth and diminishing resources (which are global issues), you might be pressured to limit your fertility by using birth control. In fact, women's ability to choose whether or not to have children has often been connected to larger historical forces. Historically, when nationalism swells, it often coincides with attempts to curb women's access to birth control. Nationalism is a sense of membership in a state and pride in that membership that's often expressed by symbols and ideologies. In its extreme forms, nationalism becomes very much

> **NATIONALISM**
>
> *n.* /ˈnash-nə-ˌli-zəm/
>
> Intense loyalty and devotion to one's nation.

focused on racial and ethnic purity, as in Nazi Germany. In these situations, women of "pure" racial and ethnic backgrounds are encouraged to have more children in order to strengthen the nation; thus, their ability to use birth control to limit the number of children they have is restricted. In Nazi Germany, Hitler awarded prizes to women who had many children.

In these and other ways, women's bodies and their ability to reproduce become tools used in the service of larger political gains.

↖ **GO TO 148.**

156

As a woman, you'll probably have less leisure time than men do, and the free time that you do have is less likely to be completely free. If you're a woman who is in a partnership, has children, and is working full time, you're likely to find yourself working what's known in feminist theory as "the second shift." The second shift consists of the added duties of housework and childcare that become part of many working women's daily lives.

Because of the second shift, you'll find that your leisure is often contaminated, so to speak, by other activities. You're likely to find yourself watching television while folding the laundry or taking the baby and stroller along on your exercise run. Your free time will be combined with chores that are much less fun. Pure leisure, time spent truly doing nothing else but relaxing and having fun, will be harder to come by. This is true regardless of whether you work inside the home, outside the home, or both.

Even though many men have begun to contribute more to the work of running a household, men still have more leisure

time than women, regardless of whether it's pure or not. For
those without children at home, the leisure gap is about three
hours—meaning that men have on average three more hours
of leisure per week than women. But when you compare men
and women with children younger than eighteen in the home,
the gap widens to an average of five more hours of leisure time
for men.

↗ You spend part of your leisure time playing sports. **GO
  TO 146.**

↘ You don't spend time playing sports. **GO TO 147.**

157

If you live in the United States as a man, you're likely to spend considerably more time doing paid work than men in many other parts of the world (a fact that is true for women in the United States, as well). American men have been working longer hours for less pay since the 1950s. You're also less likely to take advantage of the paid vacation and leave that your employer makes available to you.

When you do spend time doing something besides working, you're more likely than women to experience pure leisure. You really can sit down on the couch and do nothing but watch TV. You might go golfing and feel no need to take the kids along or run errands on the way. If you're married, you probably enjoy an average of three to five more hours of leisure a week than your wife does, depending on whether or not you have children.

↗ You spend part of your leisure time playing sports. **GO TO 146.**

↘ You don't spend time playing sports. **GO TO 147.**

↑ ↗

158

In most countries, you're not likely, as a man, to live as long as you would if you were a woman. In the United States, it's only a gap of seven years, but in Russia, it's twelve. If you live in a developing country, the gap between your life expectancy and that of a woman will be smaller. But at all ages, you're likely to die earlier than your female counterparts. Why?

Much of the explanation for these differences lies in the way that masculinity is constructed. Like other men, you're more likely to engage in risky, dangerous behaviors. Maybe you drive faster than you should or pursue more high-risk hobbies like mountain climbing or skydiving. You might smoke cigarettes; it's only been in the latter part of the twentieth century and the twenty-first century that women's rates of smoking have caught up to those of men. Although men and women attempt suicide at the same rate, as a man, your suicide attempt is more likely to be successful, meaning that men are more likely to die as a result of their suicide attempt. This difference is mostly due to the methods used by women and men to attempt suicide. Women are more likely to use nonviolent methods such as drug overdose, while men shoot or hang themselves.

Because you feel like you have to be tough and self-sufficient as a man, you might be less likely to go to the doctor when something's wrong. That means that otherwise treatable illnesses will get caught later, when they've become more life-threatening.

Gender will also impact your health by way of your social networks. People with strong social support networks have better health outcomes. Men's networks tend to be larger and composed of more nonkin connections—more people from outside your family. That sort of network is helpful for things like finding a job, starting your own business, or landing a promotion. But it's less helpful at providing you with the kind of emotional and psychological support that can be crucial when you're battling an illness. A lack of supportive networks becomes especially problematic as men age. Men who find themselves without a spouse or partner in their elderly years often lack the social networks to help them navigate the declining health that can come with growing old.

↖ **GO TO 148.**

159

As a woman, you're likely to live longer than men. From an early age, your gender can impact your health. A historic preference for sons over daughters still persists in some places today, and that can sometimes mean that more resources are directed toward boys. That's especially true in places like China, where female fetuses are often aborted and girls are sometimes abandoned as babies or given up for adoption. A preference for sons can often be subtler, shaping the way that resources are distributed between sons and daughters. These cultural beliefs about gender (that sons are more valuable than daughters) can have physical, bodily effects too.

For example, these beliefs can contribute to whether you're taller or shorter than men. How tall you are depends partly on genetics, but it also has to do with nutrition. In the past, and still in some places, feeding sons takes higher priority over feeding daughters. However, height differences between women and men have been converging in developed countries over time. Women are getting taller, and that has to do with how daughters are treated by their families. When more daughters get better nutrition from their families, women will grow taller over time. In this way, gender beliefs actually shape how gender plays out physically in the bodies of women and men.

Despite this preference for sons over daughters worldwide, you're still probably going to live longer as a woman. Women are less likely to engage in risky and life-threatening behaviors. The riskiest behavior that you'll engage in as a woman is most likely to be giving birth, and the dangers associated with childbirth have decreased over time.

You'll also live longer as a woman because of the kind of work that you do. Men are more likely to work in jobs that are dangerous and take a toll on their bodies. Statistically, you're less likely to work in such risky professions as police officer, military member, or firefighter. There's also a lower chance that your job exposes you to toxic substances. In fact, labor laws might specifically prohibit you from working certain jobs because of the risk to potential pregnancy. Even though men's exposure to toxic substances can still cause birth defects in their children, labor laws are unlikely to protect them from such hazards.

You'll live longer as a woman, but that doesn't mean that your gender won't impact your experiences with your health in other ways.

↗ You go to the doctor for a checkup or some other health issue. **GO TO 149.**

↘ You go to the doctor for birth control. **GO TO 150.**

160

As a transgender person, you might face a unique set of issues in regard to your health. You might experience discrimination and hostility inside the doctor's office because of your gender-expansive identity. As in many other areas of life, being transgender can make you vulnerable to these sorts of stressful interactions, even when all you want is some help with a stuffed-up nose. Take the experience of one transgender patient who went to the emergency room for an asthma attack. In the exam room, the doctor called in colleagues, saying, "Take a look at this." Or the experience of another transgender patient who reported overhearing the receptionist insisting that they had to be either male or female and asking, "Which one is it?"

You'll potentially face the same set of anxieties in the doctor's office as you do in other settings. Will the doctors and nurses use the correct pronouns and your correct name? Given that they'll have access to your medical records and to the information from physical examinations and tests, will they insist on treating you as the wrong gender?

In addition, if you use hormone therapy or have had

gender-confirming surgery, you might have special health issues that not all doctors are equipped to deal with. You might struggle to find a doctor who is both accepting of your transgender status and able to help you with your unique set of health issues.

↖ **GO TO 148.**

161

You'd like to imagine something completely different! Maybe your world incorporates some aspects of gender as we know it, or maybe it has nothing in common with existing systems of gender. Maybe you imagine a world full of formless blobs, and how could formless blobs have a gender? (Though you might be surprised to find out just how gendered formless blobs can be.) Maybe it's a world where we're nothing but free-floating consciousness. Could our consciousness be gendered? What if it's a world full of robots or artificial intelligence? Would there be gender then?

You're looking for a gender possibility that no one's even thought of yet. Cool! You're ready to begin creating your own new and exciting gender path!

↗ Pick a different gender ending: **TURN TO 148.**

↘ Or **KEEP READING** to check out the conclusion.

↑   ↗

CONCLUSION

You've come to the end of your gender journey. Or have you? One book, even a book as great as this one, can't cover everything there is to know about gender. All the paths laid out in this book are best guesses about how gender might unfold, based on a body of social science research. They don't imply that everyone's journey will look the same. Just because a path leads in a certain direction in this book doesn't mean that it always works that way for people in the real world. And the many branching paths laid out here don't even begin to reflect the real complexity of gender as it's lived on a day-to-day basis, and especially as it intersects with other identities like race, social class, age, and nationality, to name just a few. That's because, in reality, there are infinite gender paths, and each of them is totally unique.

So your gender journey isn't really over. You could easily spend a lifetime learning about gender and still not know everything. That might seem discouraging, but it's also pretty exciting. You haven't come to the end of your journey because there's always the possibility of something completely new and surprising around the next corner. You can keep exploring gender and how it intersects with other parts of your experience. You can seek out information about the gender experiences of people who are very different from you. You can choose to keep moving.

Hopefully this book has helped you to see that you are, in fact, on a journey. You always have been, whether you knew it or not. Gender isn't something solid and unmoving. It's shifty, like water that's constantly flowing. Or gender is a world that's in a state of constant transformation, like a magical realm. Gender is an epic adventure.

Maybe after reading this book, you'll decide that you want to become someone who helps determine what the terrain of gender will be like in the future. As we've seen throughout our journey, although it can be fun to explore the complexities of gender in this create-a-path book format, our actual gendered lives have serious consequences. Gender as a social system is the cause of widespread inequalities.

> **GENDER OUTLAW**
>
> *n.* /ˈjen-dər ˈaůt-ˌlȯ/
>
> Someone who breaks all the gender rules society has established.

Because of gender, people sometimes lose their jobs, their families, their health, their safety and sense of well-being, and, in the very worst case scenario, their lives. Gender is much more than just a game.

↑ ↗

Because of that sometimes life-or-death aspect of gender, you might decide to become a gender outlaw, or someone who breaks all the gender rules that society lays out for us. Every day there are new attempts to push back the progress we've made so far at loosening the grip of gender on our lives. Maybe these attempts are the very last gasp of those people who want to use hatred and fear to gather power for themselves. As a gender outlaw, you'll find plenty of new work to do in order to keep us moving forward in our larger gender journey. Maybe you want to guide people along their own gender paths, or become a trailblazer, making whole safe and new tracks for those who come behind you.

Wherever you take your gender journey next, you'll know that there are always more questions to be asked. There are always more complexities to explore. There's always a new branch in the trail up ahead. Here's to fun and safe journeys ahead for all of us!

ADDITIONAL RESOURCES

American Men's Studies Association
www.mensstudies.org

The Asexual Visibility and Education Network (AVEN)
www.asexuality.org

Bitch Media
www.bitchmedia.org

Black Girl Dangerous
www.bgdblog.org

Black Lives Matter
www.blacklivesmatter.com

Center for the Study of Men and Masculinities
www.stonybrook.edu/commcms/csmm

Everyday Feminism
www.everydayfeminism.com

Feminist Frequency
www.feministfrequency.com

Feministing
www.feministing.com

Geek Feminism Wiki
www.geekfeminism.wikia.com/wiki/Geek_Feminism_Wiki

Gender Spectrum
www.genderspectrum.org

GLAAD (Gay and Lesbian Alliance Against Defamation)
www.glaad.org

GLMA: Health Professionals Advancing LGBT Equality
www.glma.org

GLSEN (Gay, Lesbian, and Straight Education Network)
www.glsen.org

The Good Men Project
www.goodmenproject.com

Intersex Society of North America (ISNA)
www.isna.org

Kiva–Women
www.kiva.org/lend/women

Men Against Violence Against Women
www.mavaw.org

Men Can Stop Rape
www.mencanstoprape.org

National Center for Transgender Equality (NCTE)
www.transequality.org

NCADV (National Coalition Against Domestic Violence)
www.ncadv.org

OII Intersex Network (Organizational Intersex International)
www.oiiinternational.com

RAINN (Rape, Abuse, and Incest National Network)
www.rainn.org

The Society Pages: *Feminist Reflections*
www.thesocietypages.org/feminist

The Society Pages: *Girl w/Pen*
www.thesocietypages.org/girlwpen

Trans Student Educational Resources (TSER)
www.transstudent.org

The Trevor Project
www.thetrevorproject.org

UN Women
www.unwomen.org

The WAGE Project
www.wageproject.org

"Why Gender Equality Is Good for Everyone—Men Included,"
TEDWomen talk by Michael Kimmel
www.ted.com/talks/michael_kimmel_why_gender_equality_is_good_for
_everyone_men_included

Women's March
www.womensmarch.com

World Professional Association for Transgender Health (WPATH)
www.wpath.org

The Youth and Gender Media Project
www.youthandgendermediaproject.org

NOTES

"Estimates vary because" M. A. Blackless et al., "How Sexually Dimorphic Are We? Review and Synthesis," *American Journal of Human Biology* 12, no. 2 (2000): 151–156.

"For comparison, that's" Rachael Rettner, "5 Health Risks of Being a Redhead," LiveScience, August 22, 2013, https://www.livescience.com/39095-redhead-health-risks.html.

"Maybe like Tonë" Serena Nanda, Gender Diversity: *Crosscultural Variations* (Long Grove, IL: Waveland Press, Inc., 2000).

"Estimates suggest that" Elena Becatoros, "Tradition of 'Sworn Virgins' Dying Out in Albania," Welt, October 6, 2008, https://www.welt.de/english-news/article2536539/Tradition-of-sworn-virgins-dying-out-in-Albania.html.

"One anthropologist suggests" Salvatore Cucchiari, "The Gender Revolution and the Transition from the Bisexual Horde to the Patrilocal Band: The Origins of Gender Hierarchy," in *Sexual Meanings: The Cultural Construction of Gender and Sexuality*, eds. Sherry B. Ortner and Harriet Whitehead (New York: Cambridge University Press, 1981).

"Part of these" James G. Peoples, "The Cultural Construction of Gender and Manhood," in *Men and Masculinity: A Text Reader*, ed. Theodore F. Cohen (Stanford, CT: Wadsworth, 2001).

"In the first" Emily Anthes, "Stretch Marks for Dad," Slate, June 14, 2007, http://www.slate.com/articles/health_and_science/medical_examiner/2007/06/stretch_marks_for_dads.html.

"She lived as" Anne Fausto-Sterling, "The Five Sexes: Why Male and Female Are Not Enough," *The Sciences*, March–April 1993.

"You'll probably find" Janell Ross, "How Easy Is It to Change the Sex

on Your Birth Certificate?" *The Washington Post*, May 18, 2016, https://www.washingtonpost.com/news/the-fix/wp/2016/05/18 /the-next-frontier-in-the-bathroom-law-debate-changing-birth -certificates/?utm_term=.f4c303469dde.

"The rules for" Lambda Legal, FAQ about Identity Documents, Lambda Legal, accessed March 28, 2018, https://www.lambdalegal.org/know -your-rights/article/trans-identity-document-faq.

"The word homosexual*"* David Halperin, *One Hundred Years of Homosexuality: And Other Essays on Greek Love* (New York: Routledge Press, 1990), 15.

"Like many ideas" Michael S. Kimmel, "Masculinity as Homophobia: Fear, Shame, and Silence on the Construction of Gender Identity," in *The Social Construction of Difference and Inequality: Race, Class, Gender and Sexuality*, ed. Tracy E. Ore (New York: McGraw Hill, 2009).

"Make a lot" Kimmel, "Masculinity as Homophobia."

"According to the" Gender Inequality Index: Table 5, United Nations Development Programme, accessed March 21, 2018, http://hdr .undp.org/en/composite/GII.

"…and on the" Global Gender Gap Report, World Economic Forum, accessed March 21, 2018, http://reports.weforum.org/global-gender-gap-report-2016 /rankings/?doing_wp_cron=1519573231.2539539337158203125000.

"In Syria, women" Gender Inequality Index.

"Fortunately, Ruqayya and" United Nations Population Fund, "I Thought I Might Die: Pregnant Women Struggle to Access Care in Embattled Syria," July 26, 2017, http://www.unfpa.org/news/i-thought-i-might -die-pregnant-women-struggle-access-care-embattled-syria.

"Some of the" Gender Inequality Index.

"But even in" Gender Inequality Index.

"Reports suggest that" "Child Marriage and the Syrian Conflict: 7 Things You Need to Know," Girls Not Brides, June 20, 2017, https:// www.girlsnotbrides.org/child-marriage-and-the-syrian-conflict-7 -things-you-need-to-know/.

"Only 12 percent" Gender Inequality Index.

"According to the" Gender Inequality Index.

"…while on the" Global Gender Gap Report.

"Unlike other countries" Nina Martin and Renee Montagne, "U.S. Has the Worst Rate of Maternal Deaths in the Developed World," NPR, May 12, 2017, http://www.npr.org/2017/05/12/528098789 /u-s-has-the-worst-rate-of-maternal-deaths-in-the-developed-world.

"There are lots" Martin and Montagne, "U.S. Has the Worst Rate of Maternal Deaths."

"As far as" Gender Inequality Index.

"The United States" Women in National Parliaments, Inter-Parliamentary Union, accessed March 21, 2018, http://archive.ipu.org/wmn-e/classif.htm.

"As of this" "Women in the U.S. House of Representatives 2018," Rutgers, accessed March 21, 2018, http://www.cawp.rutgers.edu /women-us-house-representatives-2018.

"Some of these" Gender Inequality Index.

"You've also achieved" Gender Inequality Index.

"Your country is" Global Gender Gap Report.

"Your ranking according" Gender Inequality Index.

"Looking just at" Women in National Parliaments.

"Educational attainment is" Gender Inequality Index.

"Although both women" Hanna Rosin, "Read the Transcript," *Invisibilia*, NPR, July 29, 2016, https://www.npr.org/2016/07/29/487807747 /read-the-transcript.

"Women in Rwanda" Gender Inequality Index.

"Women in your" Rosin, "Transcript."

"They changed marriage" Danielle Paquette, "Rwanda Is Beating the United States in Gender Equality," *The Washington Post*, November 20, 2015, https://www.washingtonpost.com/news/wonk /wp/2015/11/20/rwanda-is-beating-the-united-states-in-gender -equality/?utm_term=.af816327e599.

"Women like this" Rosin, "Transcript."

"There are thirteen" Siobhan Fenton, "LGBT Relationships Are Illegal in 74 Countries, Research Finds," *Independent*, May 17, 2016, http://www.independent.co.uk/news/world/gay-lesbian-bisexual -relationships-illegal-in-74-countries-a7033666.html.

"Across the globe" Dan Barry, "Realizing It's a Small, Terrifying World After All," *New York Times*, June 20, 2016, https://www.nytimes.com/2016/06/21/us/orlando-shooting-america.html?rref=collection%2Fnewseventcollection%2F2016-orlando-shooting&action=click&contentCollection=us&region=rank&module=package&version=highlights&contentPlacement=1&pgtype=collection.

"For example, one" Kirsten Schilt, *Just One of the Guys: Transgender Men and the Persistence of Gender Inequality* (Chicago: University of Chicago Press, 2010).

"One intersex woman" Sharon Preves, *Intersex and Identity: The Contested Self* (New Brunswick, NJ: Rutgers University Press, 2003).

"Online discussion pages" "TransDIY," Reddit thread, accessed March 21, 2018, https://www.reddit.com/r/TransDIY/.

"In 2017, 647" Lenny Bernstein, "Here's How Sex Reassignment Surgery Works," *The Washington Post*, February 9, 2015, https://www.washingtonpost.com/news/to-your-health/wp/2015/02/09/heres-how-sex-reassignment-surgery-works/?utm_term=.fc2c0f580053.

"In 2016, twenty-two" Human Rights Campaign Foundation, "Violence Against the Transgender Community in 2017," accessed March 21, 2018, https://www.hrc.org/resources/violence-against-the-transgender-community-in-2017.

"One physician at" Schilt, *Just One of the Guys*.

"They now require" World Professional Association for Transgender Health, *Standards of Care for the Health of Transsexual, Transgender, and Gender Nonconforming People*, 7th ed., 60.

"As of 2015" Jason Gale, "How Thailand Became a Global Gender-Change Destination," *Bloomberg*, October 26, 2015, https://www.bloomberg.com/news/features/2015-10-26/how-thailand-became-a-global-gender-change-destination.

"You might assume" Human Rights Campaign Foundation, "Marriage Equality Around the World," accessed March 21, 2018, https://assets2.hrc.org/files/assets/resources/WorldMarriageMap.pdf?_ga=2.62520364.1653054982.1520179599-1992263507.1519223850.

"During the Ming" Bonnie Zimmerman and George Haggerty, eds.

Encyclopedia of Lesbian and Gay Histories and Cultures (New York: Routledge, 1999) 163–164.

"Here's how the" John Stoltenberg, *Refusing to Be a Man: Essays on Sex and Justice* (New York: Routledge, 2000).

"We try to" Stoltenberg, *Refusing to Be a Man.*

"If the first" Naomi Wolf, *The Beauty Myth: How Images of Beauty Are Used Against Women* (New York: Harper Perennial, 2002).

"As far as" Elizabeth Denton, "How Much the Average Woman Spends on Makeup in Her Life," *Allure*, March 29, 2017, https://www.allure.com/story/average-woman-spends-on-makeup.

"As recently as" Lisa Ko, "Unwanted Sterilization and Eugenics Programs in the United States," PBS, January 29, 2016, http://www.pbs.org/independentlens/blog/unwanted-sterilization-and-eugenics-programs-in-the-united-states.

"Here's a list" Erving Goffman, *Stigma: Notes on the Management of Spoiled Identity* (Upper Saddle River, NJ: Prentice Hall, 1963), 128.

"The one-child policy" Tom Phillips, "China Ends One-Child Policy after 35 Years," *The Guardian*, October 29, 2015, https://www.theguardian.com/world/2015/oct/29/china-abandons-one-child-policy.

"In China, 48.55" Didi Kirsten Tatlow, "In China, a Lonely Valentine's Day for Millions of Men," *New York Times*, February 14, 2017, https://www.nytimes.com/2017/02/14/world/asia/china-men-marriage-gender-gap.html.

"By 2020, thirty" X. Jin et al., "'Bare Branches' and the Marriage Market in Rural China: Preliminary Evidence from a Village-Level Survey." *Chinese Sociological Review* 46, no. 1 (2013): 83–104.

"This is higher" Louise Corselli-Nordblad and Andrea Gereoffy, "Marriage and Birth Statistics: New Ways of Living Together in the EU," Eurostat, data extracted June 2015, accessed March 21, 2018, http://ec.europa.eu/eurostat/statistics-explained/index.php/Marriage_and_birth_statistics_-_new_ways_of_living_together_in_the_EU.

"Many of the" Population Europe Resource Finder & Archive, "Family Policies: Denmark (2014)," accessed March 31, 2018, http://www.perfar.eu/policy/family-children/denmark.

"Currently, the average" Eleanor Barkhorn, "Getting Married Later Is Great for College-Educated Women," *The Atlantic*, March 15, 2013, https://www.theatlantic.com/sexes/archive/2013/03/getting-married-later-is-great-for-college-educated-women/274040/.

"As Nadine Naber" Nadine Naber, "Arab American Femininities: Beyond Arab Virgin / American(ized) Whore," *Feminist Studies* 32, no. 1 (2006): 87–111.

"When researchers ask" Lisa Wade, *American Hookup: The New Culture of Sex on Campus* (New York: W. W. Norton & Company, 2017).

"Some estimates suggest" David Wessel, "The Typical Male U.S. Worker Earned Less in 2014 Than in 1973," Brookings, September 18, 2015, https://www.brookings.edu/opinions/the-typical-male-u-s-worker-earned-less-in-2014-than-in-1973/.

"Since 1970, men's" Michael Greenstone and Adal Looney, "The Uncomfortable Truth About American Wages." *New York Times*, October 22, 2012, https://economix.blogs.nytimes.com/2012/10/22/the-uncomfortable-truth-about-american-wages/?mcubz=0&_r=1.

"In fact, estimates" United Nations, "The World's Women 2015: Work," accessed March 6, 2018, https://unstats.un.org/unsd/gender/chapter4/chapter4.html.

"Only 7 percent" Gretchen Livingston, "The Likelihood of Being a Stay-at-Home Father," Pew Research Center, June 5, 2014, http://www.pewsocialtrends.org/2014/06/05/chapter-1-the-likelihood-of-being-a-stay-at-home-father/.

"Today, men take" "Gender Equality in Sweden," Sweden, last modified February 1, 2018, https://sweden.se/society/gender-equality-in-sweden/; Jareen Imam, "Sweden Moves to Extend Paid Paternity Leave for Dads," CNN, last modified May 30, 2015, https://www.cnn.com/2015/05/30/living/sweden-paid-paternity-leave/index.html.

"Two years after" S. H., "Why Swedish Men Take So Much Paternity Leave," *The Economist*, July 23, 2014, https://www.economist.com/blogs/economist-explains/2014/07/economist-explains-15.

"In Sweden, women's" S. H., "Why Swedish Men Take So Much Paternity Leave."

"Mothers spend on" Pew Research Center, "Another Gender Gap: Men Spend More Time in Leisure Activities," June 10, 2013, http://www .pewresearch.org/fact-tank/2013/06/10/another-gender-gap-men -spend-more-time-in-leisure-activities/.

"Before that, all" Randy Hodson and Teresa A. Sullivan, *The Social Organization of Work* (Stamford, CT: Wadsworth, 1990).

"Employers generally don't" Sarah Jane Glynn, "Breadwinning Mothers Are Increasingly the U.S. Norm," Center for American Progress, December 19, 2016, https://www.americanprogress.org/issues /women/reports/2016/12/19/295203/breadwinning-mothers-are -increasingly-the-u-s-norm/.

"After the transition" Schilt, *Just One of the Guys.*

"Unlike your white" Adia Harvey Wingfield, "Racializing the Glass Escalator: Reconsidering Men's Experiences with Women's Work," *Gender & Society* 23, no. 1 (2009): 5–26.

"In a famous" "Sojourner's Words and Music," Sojourner Truth Memorial Committee, accessed March 21, 2018, http://sojourner truthmemorial.org/sojourner-truth/her-words/.

"But when she" Schilt, *Just One of the Guys.*

"If you're an" American Association of University Women, *The Simple Truth About the Gender Pay Gap* (Spring 2018), accessed March 7, 2018. https://www.aauw.org/aauw_check/pdf_download/show_pdf.php ?file=The-Simple-Truth.

"Lawyers, only 36" Jennifer Pierce, "Emotional Labor Among Paralegals," *The Annals of the American Academy of Political and Social Science* 561, no. 1 (1999): 127–142.

"Tennis is one" Joshua Barajas, "Equal Pay for Equal Play: What the Sport of Tennis Got Right," PBS, April 12, 2016, https://www.pbs.org/newshour/economy/equal-pay-for-equal-play -what-the-sport-of-tennis-got-right.

"In 2017, Sylvia" David Berri, "Basketball's Growing Gender Wage Gap: The Evidence the WNBA Is Underpaying Players," *Forbes,* September 20, 2017, https://www.forbes.com/sites/davidberri/2017 /09/20/there-is-a-growing-gender-wage-gap-in-professional

-basketball/#3d2cb39f36e0; http://www.businessinsider.com/stephen-curry-salary-taxes-nba-2017-9.

"Women playing professional" Kayla Lombardo, "The Surprisingly Difficult Life of Professional Softball Players," Excelle Sports, January 6, 2017, http://www.excellesports.com/news/npf-softball-offseason-professional/.

"That's compared to" "MLB Salaries 2017: Earnings Flatten Out, while Clayton Kershaw Leads Pack," *USA Today*, April 2, 2017, https://www.usatoday.com/story/sports/mlb/2017/04/02/mlb-salaries-payroll-2017/99960994/.

"As an engineer" Bureau of Labor Statistics, Table 39, Median Weekly Earnings of Full-Time Wage and Salary Workers by Detailed Occupations and Sex, United States Department of Labor, 2016, accessed September 7, 2017, https://www.bls.gov/cps/cpsaat39.htm.

"Veterinarians will make" Bureau of Labor Statistics, Table 39.

"As recently as" Michael Pavitt, "IAAF Hope to Have Revised Hyperandrogenism Regulations in Place by November," Inside the Games, March 6, 2018, https://www.insidethegames.biz/index.php/articles/1062306/iaaf-hope-to-have-revised-hyperandrogenism-regulations-in-place-by-november.

"These declines are" Lawrence B. Finer and Stanley K. Henshaw, "Abortion Incidence and Services in the U.S. in 2000," *Perspectives on Sexual and Reproductive Health* 35, no. 1 (January/February 2004): 6–15.

"Eleven doctors and" Liam Stack, "A Brief History of Deadly Attacks on Abortion Providers," *New York Times*, November 29, 2015, https://www.nytimes.com/interactive/2015/11/29/us/30abortion-clinic-violence.html; National Abortion Federation, "NAF Violence and Disruption Statistics," accessed March 21, 2018, http://5aa1b2xfmfh2e2mk03kk8rsx.wpengine.netdna-cdn.com/wp-content/uploads/Stats_Table_2014.pdf.

"Five states have" Rebecca Harrington and Skye Gould, "The Number of Abortion Clinics in the U.S. Has Plunged in the Last Decade—Here's How Many Are in Each State," *Business Insider*,

February 10, 2017, http://www.businessinsider.com/how-many-abortion -clinics-are-in-america-each-state-2017-2.

"But when you" Pew Research Center, "Another Gender Gap: Men Spend More Time in Leisure Activities."

"If you're married" Pew Research Center, "Another Gender Gap: Men Spend More Time in Leisure Activities."

"If you live" Rosamund Hutt, "In Which Countries Do Women Outlive Men by More Than a Decade?" World Economic Forum, May 20, 2016, https://www.weforum.org/agenda/2016/05/countries -where-women-outlive-men-by-decade/; Bertrand Desjardins, "Why Is Life Expectancy Longer for Women Than It Is for men?" *Scientific American*, accessed March 6, 2018, https://www.scientificamerican .com/article/why-is-life-expectancy-lo/.

"Take the experience" Liz Kowalcyk, "In Mass., Transgender Patients Decry Hostility Over Medical Care," *Boston Globe*, February 1, 2017, https://www.bostonglobe.com/metro/2017/02/01/transgender-people -say-hostility-ignorance-common-doctors-offices-emergency-rooms /HYfNoCi2HAHw1QANBJnMJP/story.html.

BIBLIOGRAPHY

American Association of University Women (AAUW). *The Simple Truth about the Gender Pay Gap*. Washington, DC: AAUW, 2017. https://www.aauw.org/aauw_check/pdf_download/show_pdf .php?file=The-Simple-Truth.

Anthes, Emily. "Stretch Marks for Dad." Slate. June 14, 2007. http:// www.slate.com/articles/health_and_science/medical_examiner /2007/06/stretch_marks_for_dads.html.

Bailey, Beth L. *From Front Porch to Back Seat: Courtship in Twentieth-Century America*. Baltimore, MD: John Hopkins University Press, 1989.

Barkhorn, Eleanor. "Getting Married Later Is Great for College-Educated Women." *The Atlantic*. March 15, 2013. https://www.theatlantic .com/sexes/archive/2013/03/getting-married-later-is-great-for -college-educated-women/274040/.

Bernstein, Lenny. "Here's How Sex Reassignment Surgery Works." *The Washington Post*. February 9, 2015. https://www.washingtonpost .com/news/to-your-health/wp/2015/02/09/heres-how-sex -reassignment-surgery-works/?utm_term=.fc2c0f580053.

Berry, Dan. "Realizing It's a Small, Terrifying World After All." *The New York Times*. June 20, 2016. https://www.nytimes.com/2016/06/21/us /orlando-shooting-america.html?rref=collection%2Fnewsevent collection%2F2016-orlando-shooting&action=click&content Collection=us&region=rank&module=package&version=high lights&contentPlacement=1&pgtype=collection.

Blackless, M., A. Charuvastra, A. Fausto-Sterling, K. Lauzanne, and E. Lee. "How Sexually Dimorphic Are We? Review and Synthesis." *American Journal of Human Biology* 12, no. 2 (2000): 151–156.

Bornstein, Kate. *Gender Outlaw: On Men, Women and the Rest of Us*. New York: Vintage, 1995.

Branstetter, Gillian. 2016. "Sketchy Pharmacies Are Selling Hormones to Transgender People." *The Atlantic*. August 31, 2016. https://www .theatlantic.com/health/archive/2016/08/diy-hormone -replacement-therapy/498044/.

Bureau of Labor Statistics. Table 39. "Median Weekly Earnings of Full-Time Wage and Salary Workers by Detailed Occupations and Sex." Last modified January 19, 2018. Accessed September 7, 2017. United States Department of Labor, Washington, DC. https://www.bls .gov/cps/cpsaat39.htm.

Chodorow, Nancy. *The Reproduction of Mothering: Psychoanalysis and the Sociology of Gender*. Berkeley, CA: University of California Press, 1999.

Corselli-Nordblad, Louise and Andrea Gereoffy. "Marriage and Birth Statistics: New Ways of Living Together in the EU." Eurostat. Data extracted June 2015. Accessed March 6, 2018. http://ec .europa.eu/eurostat/statistics-explained/index.php/Marriage _and_birth_statistics_-_new_ways_of_living_together_in_the _EU.

Cucchiari, Salvatore. "The Gender Revolution and the Transition from the Bisexual Horde to the Patrilocal Band: The Origins of Gender Hierarchy." In *Sexual Meanings: The Cultural Construction of Gender and Sexuality*, edited by Sherry B. Ortner and Harriet Whitehead. New York: Cambridge University Press, 1981.

Denton, Elizabeth. 2017. "How Much the Average Woman Spends on Makeup in Her Life." *Allure*. March 29, 2017. https://www.allure .com/story/average-woman-spends-on-makeup.

Desjardins, Bertrand. "Why Is Life Expectancy Longer for Women Than It Is for Men?" *Scientific American*. 2004. Accessed March 6, 2018. https:// www.scientificamerican.com/article/why-is-life-expectancy-lo/.

DiProperzio, Linda. "Should You Raise a Gender-Neutral Baby?" *Parents*. 2013. Accessed September 6, 2017. http://www.parents.com /parenting/gender-neutral-parenting/.

The Economist. "Why Swedish Men Take So Much Paternity Leave." July 23, 2014. https://www.economist.com/blogs/economist -explains/2014/07/economist-explains-15.

Engels, Friedrich. *The Origin of the Family, Private Property and the State.* New York: Penguin Classics, 2010.

Fausto-Sterling, Anne. "The Five Sexes: Why Male and Female Are Not Enough." *The Sciences* (March–April 1993).

———. "The Five Sexes, Revisited." *The Sciences* (July–August 2000).

Fenton, Siobhan. "LGBT Relationships Are Illegal in 74 Countries, Research Finds." *The Independent.* May 17, 2016. http://www.independent .co.uk/news/world/gay-lesbian-bisexual-relationships-illegal-in -74-countries-a7033666.html.

Finer, Lawrence B. and Stanley K. Henshaw. "Abortion Incidence and Services in the U.S. in 2000." *Perspectives on Sexual and Reproductive Health* 35, no. 1 (January–February 2004): 6–15.

Frost, Natasha. "For Centuries, People Celebrated a Little Boy's First Pair of Trousers." Atlas Obscura. September 18, 2017. https://www.atlasobscura .com/articles/breeching-party-first-pants-regency-trousers-boys.

Gale, Jason. "How Thailand Became a Global Gender-Change Destination." *Bloomberg.* October 26, 2015. https://www.bloomberg.com/ news/features/2015-10-26/how-thailand-became-a-global-gender -change-destination.

Gerschick, Thomas J. "Toward a Theory of Disability and Gender." *Signs: Journal of Women in Culture and Society* 25, no. 4 (Summer 2000): 1263–1268.

Gholipour, Bahar. 2014. "5 Ways Fatherhood Changes a Man's Brain." LiveScience. June 14, 2014. https://www.livescience.com/46322 -fatherhood-changes-brain.html.

Gilligan, Carol. *In a Different Voice: Psychological Theory and Women's Development.* Boston: Harvard University Press, 2016.

Girls Not Brides. "Child Marriage and the Syrian Conflict: 7 Things You Need to Know." Girls Not Brides. June 20, 2017. https://www .girlsnotbrides.org/child-marriage-and-the-syrian-conflict-7 -things-you-need-to-know/.

Glynn, Sarah Jane. 2016. "Breadwinning Mothers Are Increasingly the U.S. Norm." Center for American Progress. December 19, 2016. https://www.americanprogress.org/issues/women/reports/2016/12/19/295203/breadwinning-mothers-are-increasingly-the-u-s-norm/.

Goettner-Abendroth, Heidi and Karen P. Smith. "Matriarchies as Societies of Peace: Re-thinking Matriarchy." *Off Our Backs* 38, no. 1 (January 2008): 49–52.

Goffman, Erving. *Stigma*. New Jersey: Prentice Hall, 1963.

Goldsztajin, Iris. "12 Gender-Neutral Clothing Brands You Need to Know About." Her Campus. January 31, 2017. https://www.hercampus.com/style/12-gender-neutral-clothing-brands-you-need-know-about.

Greenstone, Michael and Adal Looney. "The Uncomfortable Truth about American Wages." *New York Times*. October 22, 2012. https://economix.blogs.nytimes.com/2012/10/22/the-uncomfortable-truth-about-american-wages/?mcubz=0&_r=1.

Halperin, David. *One Hundred Years of Homosexuality: And Other Essays on Greek Love*. New York: Routledge Press, 1990.

Hanna, Bo. "This Is What It's Like to Raise Gender-Neutral Children." VICE. April 5, 2016. https://www.vice.com/en_us/article/ppxjvb/raising-children-genderneutral-876.

Haselhuhn, M. P., E. M. Wong, and M. E. Ormiston. Self-Fulfilling Prophecies as a Link between Men's Facial Width-to-Height Ratio and Behavior. PLoS ONE 8, no. 8 (2013): https://doi.org/10.1371/journal.pone.0072259.

Hodson, Randy and Teresa A. Sullivan. *The Social Organization of Work*. Stamford, CT: Wadsworth, 1990.

Hoschild, Arlie. *The Managed Heart: The Commercialization of Human Feeling*. Berkeley, CA: University of California Press, 2012.

———. *The Second Shift: Working Families and the Revolution at Home*. New York: Penguin Books, 2012.

Hosi, Rachel. "What Is Demisexuality?" *The Independent*. August 28, 2017. http://www.independent.co.uk/life-style/love-sex/demisexuality

-what-is-it-sex-orientation-emotional-relationships-physical
-a7912661.html.

Human Rights Campaign. "Corporate Equality Index 2017: Rating Workplaces on Lesbian, Gay, Bisexual and Transgender Equality." Human Rights Campaign. January 4, 2017. http://www.hrc.org /resources/corporate-equality-index-list-of-businesses-with -transgender-inclusive-heal.

———. "Violence Against the Transgender Community in 2017." Human Rights Campaign. Accessed March 1, 2018. https://www.hrc.org /resources/violence-against-the-transgender-community-in-2017.

———. "Marriage Equality Around the World." Last modified January 2018. https://assets2.hrc.org/files/assets/resources/WorldMarriage Map.pdf?_ga=2.62520364.1653054982.1520179599-19922 63507.1519223850.

Hutt, Rosamund. 2016. "In Which Countries Do Women Outlive Men by More Than a Decade?" World Economic Forum. May 20, 2016. https://www.weforum.org/agenda/2016/05/countries-where -women-outlive-men-by-decade/.

Inter-parliamentary Union. "Women in National Parliaments." Last modified January 1, 2018. http://www.ipu.org/wmn-e/classif.htm.

Intersex Society of North America. "Shifting the Paradigm of Intersex Treatment." Accessed September 6, 2017. http://www.isna.org/compare.

Jin, X., L. Liu, Y. Li, M. W. Feldman, and S. Li. (2013). "'Bare Branches' and the Marriage Market in Rural China: Preliminary Evidence from a Village-Level Survey." *Chinese Sociological Review* 46, no. 1 (2013): 83–104.

Kane, Emily W. *The Gender Trap: Parents and the Pitfalls of Raising Boys and Girls.* New York: NYU Press, 2012.

Kang, Miliann. *The Managed Hand: Race, Gender and the Body in Beauty Service Work.* Berkeley, CA: University of California Press, 2010.

Kimmel, Michael S. "Masculinity as Homophobia: Fear, Shame, and Silence on the Construction of Gender Identity." In *The Social Construction of Difference and Inequality: Race, Class, Gender and Sexuality*, edited by Tracy E. Ore. New York: McGraw Hill, 2009.

Ko, Lisa. 2016. "Unwanted Sterilization and Eugenics Programs in the United States." PBS. January 29, 2016. http://www.pbs.org /independentlens/blog/unwanted-sterilization-and-eugenics -programs-in-the-united-states/.

Kowalcyk, Liz. 2017. "In Mass., Transgender Patients Decry Hostility over Medical Care." *Boston Globe*. February 1, 2017. https://www .bostonglobe.com/metro/2017/02/01/transgender-people-say -hostility-ignorance-common-doctors-offices-emergency-rooms /HYfNoCi2HAHw1QANBJnMJP/story.html.

Larsson, Naomi. "Is the World Finally Waking Up to Intersex Rights?" *The Guardian*. February 10, 2016. https://www.theguardian.com /global-development-professionals-network/2016/feb/10/intersex -human-rights-lgbti-chile-argentina-uganda-costa-rica.

Livingston, Gretchen. "Growing Numbers of Dads Home with Kids." Pew Research Center. June 5, 2014. http://www.pewsocialtrends.org/2014 /06/05/chapter-1-the-likelihood-of-being-a-stay-at-home-father/.

Lombardo, Kayla. "The Surprisingly Difficult Life of Professional Softball Players." Excelle Sports. January 6, 2017. http://www.excellesports .com/news/npf-softball-offseason-professional/.

Lorber, Judith. *Paradoxes of Gender*. New Haven, CT: Yale University Press, 1994.

Lucal, Betsy. "What It Means to Be Gendered Me: Life on the Boundaries of a Dichotomous Gender System." *Gender & Society* 13, no. 6 (December 1, 1999): 781–797.

Martin, Karin. *Puberty, Sexuality and the Self: Boys and Girls at Adolescence*. New Brunswick, NJ: Rutgers Press, 1996.

Martin, Nina and Renee Montagne. "U.S. Has the Worst Rate of Maternal Deaths in the Developed World." NPR. May 12, 2017. http:// www.npr.org/2017/05/12/528098789/u-s-has-the-worst-rate-of -maternal-deaths-in-the-developed-world.

Mead, Margaret. *Sex and Temperament in Three Primitive Societies*. New York: Harper Perennial, 2001.

Naber, Nadine. "Arab American Femininities: Beyond Arab Virgin / American(ized) Whore." *Feminist Studies* 32, no. 1 (2006): 87–111.

Nanda, Serena. *Neither Man Nor Woman: The* Hijras *of India.* Belmont, CA: Wadsworth Publishing, 1998.

———. *Gender Diversity: Cross-Cultural Variations.* Long Grove, IL: Waveland Press, 2014.

Oyěwùmí, Oyèrónké. *The Invention of Women: Making African Sense of Western Gender Discourses.* Minneapolis, MN: University of Minnesota Press, 1997.

Padawer, Ruth. "The Humiliating Practice of Sex Testing Female Athletes." *New York Times.* June 28, 2016. https://www.nytimes .com/2016/07/03/magazine/the-humiliating-practice-of-sex -testing-female-athletes.html?mcubz=0&_r=0.

Parquette, Danielle. 2015. "Rwanda Is Beating the United States in Gender Equality." *The Washington Post.* November 20, 2015. https:// www.washingtonpost.com/news/wonk/wp/2015/11/20/rwanda -is-beating-the-united-states-in-gender-equality/?utm_term= .afb7fac89b34.

Pavitt, Michael. "IAAF Hope to Have Revised Hyperandregenism Regulations in Place By November." Inside the Games. March 6, 2018. https://www.insidethegames.biz/index.php/articles /1062306/iaaf-hope-to-have-revised-hyperandrogenism -regulations-in-place-by-november.

Peoples, James G. "The Cultural Construction of Gender and Manhood." In *Men and Masculinity: A Text Reader,* edited by Theodore F. Cohen. Stanford, CT: Wadsworth, 2001.

Pew Research Center. "Another Gender Gap: Men Spend More Time in Leisure Activities." Pew Research Center. June 10, 2013. http:// www.pewresearch.org/fact-tank/2013/06/10/another-gender-gap -men-spend-more-time-in-leisure-activities/ Retrieved Nov. 7, 2017.

Pierce, Jennifer. "Emotional Labor Among Paralegals." *The Annals of the American Academy of Political and Social Science* 561, no. 1 (1999): 127–142.

Preves, Sharon. *Intersex and Identity: The Contested Self.* New Brunswick, NJ: Rutgers University Press, 2003.

Rettner, Rachel. 2013. "5 Health Risks of Being a Redhead." LiveScience.

August 22, 2013. https://www.livescience.com/39095-redhead-health-risks.html.

Rosin, Hanna. *Invisibilia: Outside In.* National Public Radio. July 29, 2016. http://www.npr.org/2016/07/29/487807747/read-the-transcript.

Schilt, Kirsten. *Just One of the Guys: Transgender Men and the Persistence of Gender Inequality.* Chicago: University of Chicago Press, 2010.

Shaw, Maureen. "Science Shows Gender Neutral Toys Empower Children, and Possibly Society at Large." Quartz. September 5, 2015. https://qz.com/494673/science-shows-gender-neutral-toys-empower-children-and-possibly-society-at-large/.

Stoltenberg, John. *Refusing to Be a Man: Essays on Sex and Justice.* New York: Routledge, 2010.

Tannen, Deborah. *You Just Don't Understand: Women and Men in Conversation.* New York: William Morrow Books, 2007.

Tølbøll, Lene. "Family Policies: Denmark." Population Europe Resource Finder & Archive. 2014. http://www.perfar.eu/policy/family-children/denmark.

Topping, Alexandra. "Rwanda's Women Make Strides Towards Equality 20 Years After Genocide." *The Guardian.* April 7, 2014. https://www.theguardian.com/global-development/2014/apr/07/rwanda-women-empowered-impoverished.

TransDIY. Reddit. Accessed December 15, 2017. https://www.reddit.com/r/TransDIY/.

Truth, Sojourner. "'Ain't I a Woman?' Speech at Women's Right Convention in Akron, 1851." Accessed March 7, 2018. http://sojournertruthmemorial.org/sojourner-truth/her-words/.

United Nations. "The World's Women 2015: Work." Accessed March 6, 2018. https://unstats.un.org/unsd/gender/chapter4/chapter4.html.

United Nations Development Programme. Table 5: Gender Inequality Index. 2015. Accessed September 6, 2017. http://hdr.undp.org/en/composite/GII.

United Nations Population Fund. "I Thought I Might Die: Pregnant Women Struggle to Access Care in Embattled Syria." United Nations Population Fund. July 26, 2017. http://www.unfpa.org

/news/i-thought-i-might-die-pregnant-women-struggle-access
-care-embattled-syria.

University of Southern California Transgender Care. "Information on Estrogen Hormone Therapy." Accessed September 7, 2017. https:// transcare.ucsf.edu/article/information-estrogen-hormone-therapy.

Viloria, Hida. *Born Both: An Intersex Life.* New York: Hachette Books, 2017.

Wade, Lisa. *American Hookup: The New Culture of Sex on Campus.* New York: W. W. Norton & Company, 2017.

Williams, Walter L. *The Spirit and the Flesh: Sexual Diversity in American Indian Culture.* Boston: Beacon Press, 1992.

Wingfield, Adia Harvey. "Racializing the Glass Escalator: Reconsidering Men's Experiences with Women's Work." *Gender & Society* 23, no. 1 (2009): 5–26.

Wolf, Naomi. *The Beauty Myth: How Images of Beauty Are Used Against Women.* New York: Harper Perennial, 2002.

World Economic Forum. The Global Gender Index Gap Rankings 2015. Accessed September 6, 2017. http://reports.weforum.org /global-gender-gap-report-2015/rankings/.

World Professional Association for Transgender Health. *Standards of Care for the Health of Transsexual, Transgender and Gender Nonconforming People*, 7th ed. 2011. Accessed March 2, 2018. https://s3.amazonaws.com/amo_hub_content/Association140 /files/Standards%20of%20Care%20V7%20-%202011%20 WPATH%20(2)(1).pdf.

Zimmerman, Bonnie and George Haggerty, eds. *Encyclopedia of Lesbian and Gay Histories and Cultures.* New York: Routledge, 1999.

ACKNOWLEDGMENTS

Some people spend years planning out every detail of their dream wedding or figuring out how they'll raise the perfect child or drawing elaborate plans for ideal the house they'll build. If you're a writer, you spend all that energy composing acknowledgments, hoping for that day when your book is finally published. Then when it comes, you're still not ready. Here it goes, anyway.

Thank you to every single person who in the least bit helped to prop up my dream of being a writer. It's a very, very long list. It includes teachers and neighbors and family and friends and fellow writers. It starts with my third-grade teacher, Mrs. Hendrickson, who liked my poem about flowers. It includes my late neighbor, John McEvoy, who read one of my stories once and liked it. It stretches to all the folks who read and commented on and told me they liked my blog.

Thank you to the town of Madison, Indiana, the perfect place to be a writer and a sociologist and just generally a person. Thank you Deb at Cocoa Safari for keeping me well-supplied in sour neon gummy worms. To Nick, Rich, Colyn, and all the other folks at Red Roaster who make me cappuccinos and have, on more than one occasion, offered to run people out of "our" spot. Thank you Nathan and Anne for running the best independent bookstore in the world—Village Lights—and for being there in every way possible for local artists.

My LASS friends—Carla, Jeni, Katy, and Sandi—thank you for looking at a very early version of this book and not telling me I was insane.

I've been lucky to have so many amazing people who've taught me about gender, inside and outside the classroom. My professors at Millsaps College and all the other kick-ass women who first showed me what feminism means. Do not mess with Southern feminists, y'all. Thank you also to my great friends and gender studies colleagues at Hanover College, Sara Patterson and Kate Johnson. Special shout out to Kate for reading an early draft. Thank you to Ellen Airgood for also reading a draft and for being my writing friend.

I could not have written this book without the years of experience in the trenches teaching college students about gender. Thank you to all those young people who helped me figure out what were the most important and interesting bits to share. A special thanks to Ashley Eden and Nicholas Jackson, who read drafts and shared their incredible wisdom with me.

Thank you to the amazing team at Sourcebooks, who didn't need to be convinced how cool this book could be and who then went about making it happen. Thank you, Grace Menary-Winefield, for all your unending enthusiasm and incredible insight. Thanks to Michelle Lecuyer and Cassie Gutman for their detailed editing and production work. This book looks as beautiful as it does thanks to the brilliant work of Zoe Norvell, Adrienne Krogh, Heather Morris, and Jillian Rahn.

This book would not have happened without the dedication and enthusiasm and just general awesomeness of Brent Taylor and the folks at Triada US Literary. I am truly proud to be represented by Brent, who is a relentless advocate for diversity in publishing and generally using books to make the world a better place for everyone.

I'm grateful to have grown up with a dad who never cared that my sister and I were girls and a mom who had very little interest in most girly things. I also can't help but believe that being the middle child—stuck between my older sister and younger brother—is part of what made me become a sociologist.

Thank you, Grace, for patiently tolerating the many sociological lectures at the dinner table.

Most of all, I'd like to thank my husband, Jeff. I grew up thinking marriage was a horrible sort of trap, and you taught me that, when you do it right, it actually sets you free. Thank you for being my first editor and for always saying yes.

ABOUT THE AUTHOR

Dr. Robyn Ryle grew up reading choose-your-own-adventure books and has more than fifteen years of experience making the topic of gender interesting and approachable. Her textbook *Questioning Gender: A Sociological Exploration* is in its third edition and has been translated into Korean. Her writing on gender inequality appears in *Investigating Social Problems* (SAGE Press, 2014) and the *Wiley-Blackwell Encyclopedia of Gender and Sexuality*. She has published essays on gender and race at Gawker, *StorySouth*, and Little Fiction/Big Truths, among others. She has a PhD in sociology from Indiana University–Bloomington and is currently professor of sociology and gender studies at Hanover College in Hanover, Indiana. In her spare time, she enjoys knitting, gardening, baking, playing music (badly), and generally enjoying small-town life. She lives in a 140-year-old house with her husband, her daughter, and two peculiar cats.